The Scholarship Résumé

Simplify Your Application & Access Your Share of Billion$

Dr. John W. Mitchell

ISBN: 1985068133
ISBN-13: 978-1985068131

DEDICATION

To my wonderful wife and kids for their ability to always find the best in everything!

Also, to all those out there who have wanted to go to college, but just felt like they couldn't afford it, this is for you - a simple tool to help you achieve your dreams.

CONTENTS

ACKNOWLEDGMENTS

I would like to thank all those who have helped me find the time and the desire to finally finish this book. I am also grateful to those who have helped me with the editing and content adjustment to make it a much more readable work: Randy Hardin, Paula Bothwell and Josh Nelson have each impacted this work for the better. Thank you!

Also, thank you to those thousands of students who have let me work with you to help make your collegiate goals a reality. When you share your challenges and victories it inspires me to do more of this kind of work.

ENDORSEMENTS

"A must-read resource for any student! John Mitchell's book *The Scholarship Résumé* opens up the 'black box' of scholarship applications making the process not only easier to master, but also shows how scholarships do not belong only to the domain of outstanding students, but are also accessible to a broad spectrum of students at different stages of study. I heartily recommend this excellent resource."

Deryck J van Rensburg, Dean, Pepperdine University, Graziadio Business School

"Having worked in Higher Education for over 20 years, the biggest barrier to entry I see for students is cost. This can be off-set to a large extent by applying for and receiving financial aid in the form of scholarships, grants, and loans.

But this can be a daunting task for new students, especially if there is no one knowledgeable that is available to guide them. A comprehensive guide like this one will give students a head start in securing the funding necessary to be successful in higher education. "

Dr. Jeffrey S. Delaney, University System of Georgia

"*The Scholarship Résumé* demystifies the college scholarship process and provides sound advice on extracurricular enhancements and positioning for success. Mitchell's book is a go-to resource in the complex world of competing for scholarships."

Libby V. Morris, Ph.D., Director, Institute of Higher Education, University of Georgia

"Dr. Mitchell has committed his career to advantage students in their educational pursuits. His passion for education supports his unparalleled drive to discover opportunities for students to excel."

Dr. Wendy E. Hoffman, Manchester University

"Given the cost and competition, it is incredibly valuable to have a strategy for scholarships. John Mitchell's "The Scholarship Resume" will better equip students, and their families, as they go through one of the most important processes in their academic careers."

Peter W. Singer, bestselling author of books like *Ghost Fleet* and *Wired for War*

"Dr. John Mitchell has a passion for making post-secondary education meet the needs of real people who want to build real careers, and it shows in this book. It's a practical and accessible guide to improving the chance for scholarship funding, and I recommend it to students, and their parents."

Congressman Jim Talent, Missouri

John Mitchell in *The Scholarship Résumé* has created a simple system for what can be a complex and frustrating process. If you are a parent or student with college on the horizon, this is the book for you. John's step-by-step approach to building references and developing your essay will save you time and frustration all while getting you closer to your scholarship goals. Get the book!

Misty Lown, Founder & Owner, More Than Just Great Dancing

"The cost of education is going through the roof! And yet, there are hundreds of millions of dollars of attainable scholarships out there for the enterprising student to access.

Finding this book is like you've just stumble across a hidden vein of gold. Herein is the blueprint for getting the scholarship you may sorely need. Being at the right college or university can set you in a path of greater success in life. So don't miss learning the secrets that John Mitchell shares in this priceless book. I strongly recommend it!!!!"

Robert Allen, #1 New York Times bestselling author

"As life becomes more competitive and complex, so has the process of receiving higher education. John Mitchell clearly places students in a power position to work through this intricate maze and emerge with a quality education at an affordable price."

Congressman Pete Sessions (TX-32), Chairman of the House of Representatives Committee on Rules

"As a father of three young children, I am extremely mindful of the rising costs of a college education. I appreciate the passion and devotion John has provided by sharing his insights and tools to help make college more affordable for those pursuing this pathway."

Jay Timmons, President and CEO, National Association of Manufacturers

"The Scholarship Résumé provides a timely, sharp analysis that serves as a field guide for the increasingly complicated scholarship acquisition process. As university tuition continues to become prohibitively expensive, Dr. Mitchell's book guides the reader through the often-convoluted, subjective methods that universities use to separate the typical resumes from the exceptional ones. Using clear, concise, and insightful language; Mitchell crafts a simple to follow, step-by-step blueprint that maximizes an applicant's success of obtaining a top-tier scholarship, while mentoring applicants on how to fully exhaust all opportunities available to them. This is a must read for students and parents alike, as the carefully curated instruction provided may very well be the difference between the student who simply gains admission to a university and the student who earns that coveted scholarship."

Congressman John Tanner, Tennessee

DR. JOHN W. MITCHELL

FORWARD

"FREE TUITION MONEY FOR COLLEGE!!! Are you kidding me...I could have applied for scholarships galore and saved tens of thousands of dollars on my education? How could I have been so naïve and uninformed! I need to tell my family and friends who want to be college bound to read *The Scholarship Résumé* and make their education more affordable now!"

I have heard students complain about their lack of knowledge regarding available scholarships often during my 35-year career as a Harvard MBA educated CEO and multiple award-winning teacher at prestigious universities, the last 15 years at The Graziadio Business School, Pepperdine University in Malibu, California. College costs continue to rise and are putting many global student prospects on the sidelines for what should be a life changing opportunity to further their education, advance their career and reach the powerful potential of their capabilities and dreams. And BILLIONS of scholarship dollars are available for both prospective and current students each year!

My good friend and fellow Graziadio Board Member, Dr. John Mitchell, is a globally recognized scholar and CEO who formerly helped award over $1 million in scholarships in a single year as CEO of Golden Key, the world's largest collegiate honor society. The Scholarship Résumé takes the mystery out of applying for scholarships while significantly increasing the likelihood of an award. Students (and their parents) will be amazed how simple Dr. Mitchell has made the application process...and delivers the exact tools needed to set the process in motion to "see the money". I especially like Chapter 9, "W is for Winner", because it takes the previous Chapter's step by step process to its logical conclusion which makes readers more likely scholarship winners.

Who better to deliver this message and unlock this massive opportunity for potential students of all kinds than Dr. Mitchell. He has been a frequent guest lecturer to my students at Graziadio's MBA Program and his warm, intelligent, energizing and engaging manner inspires students to his message and instills confidence in their discovery of all things new. He is passionate about students, their learning and their maximum success. He understands students and their needs more than any educator I have known. Students want to know why Dr. Mitchell is not a full-time member of our Faculty every time he speaks to them. They want MORE! Dr. Mitchell gives it to them with The Scholarship Résumé!

John Buckingham
Marketing Professor
Graziadio Business School
Pepperdine University
Malibu, California
January 2018

PREFACE

Before I take the time to read a book or article, I like to make sure the source is credible. I thought I should share a few reasons why you might want to spend some time reading my thoughts (I mean this book, not telepathy). At the risk of sounding like I'm tooting my own horn, I will briefly share some of the reasons I'm qualified to help you improve your chances at winning scholarships.

First, you and I likely share a similar set of school experiences. I have been a student at many different levels (high school, university undergraduate, graduate, and post-graduate), and attended different institutions for each degree. That's not all that uncommon, but I also spent a number of years as the CEO for the world's largest university honor society, where I worked with hundreds of universities, faculty and staff, and of course, thousands of students.   Finally, my doctorate degree is in higher education management from one of the top institutions in the United States. This last degree is designed to prepare candidates to run universities.

When I was at the university honor society, I would often get asked, "How can I get a scholarship?" This was likely because at that time we were awarding over $1 million in scholarships, so naturally people wanted to know. We had been working with hundreds of universities all over the world, so the varieties and differences between these universities provided even more to succeed at receiving scholarships.

Throughout my life and studies, I have found that taking a systematic approach has allowed me to be both efficient and consistent in my efforts toward achieving a goal. Given that I like to have a system (probably a holdover from my electrical engineering days), I considered the overwhelming desire of nearly every parent or student to get free money for college. The following book is a compilation of various items I have learned or experienced over the years organized into a single system – *The Scholarship Résumé*.

The first chapter "What on Earth is a Scholarship Résumé?" provides a high-level overview of what exactly a Scholarship Résumé is and how it was developed. The second chapter goes on to provide "The Make-up of a

Scholarship Résumé," where the various sections are explored in more detail. Chapters three through eight cover each of these sections of your scholarship résumé in depth, so you will better be able to build and complete your scholarship résumé. The final chapter describes how to use your scholarship résumé to win scholarship and award money!

Throughout this book you will find links to various videos and downloads that will support some of the points that I share. These links include additional tools and programs that will guarantee that you can significantly reduce college expenses by thousands of dollars! (As these are sometimes difficult to type in, I have included a references and notes section at the end of the book. This section has a web page that will provide access to click-able links as well as where to find various facts and references made in the book. Hopefully this section will ease your ability to take advantage of more of the materials and benefits of this book.)

You will soon discover that I like to share stories from my own personal experience in an informal, conversational style in an effort to help you better understand the points I am trying to make. I have used only first names or removed the names of individuals who are part of the stories, as I am sharing it from my perspective.

I hope you enjoy this work, but even more – I hope you implement my suggestions and win more scholarships and awards! I hope you join the many others who have eliminated $1,000s from their college costs by acting on the advice and suggestions provided herein.

Feel free to share your experiences with *The Scholarship Résumé*, so I can continue to improve the messages contained herein for future generations. (E-mail me at **tsr@scholarshipkeys.com** or post a comment on our Facebook page at *www.facebook.com/scholarshipkeys*.)

All the best!

Dr. John W. Mitchell

DR. JOHN W. MITCHELL

CHAPTER 1:
WHAT ON EARTH
IS A
SCHOLARSHIP
RÉSUMÉ?

The basic description of the Scholarship Résumé: what it is, how it came about, and why it will help you to access your share of the billions of dollars available in scholarships each year.

Chapter 1: What on Earth is a Scholarship Résumé?

While I was preparing to search for a new position at a particular time in my career, the crafting of my résumé became a key activity. I met with consultants and experts to help develop my résumé so it would be impeccable. One of the things I learned is that there is no *single* perfect résumé for all situations; you need to customize your résumé for each job application to increase your chances of getting out of the stacks of résumés and into an actual interview. The practicality of customizing each application results in either applying for very few jobs, or in creating a few specific résumé templates that can be tweaked for each job application.

Trying to find and win the right scholarship has strong parallels to finding the right job. There are many scholarships advertised out there on a myriad of websites and you need to find a way to sift through all those opportunities and apply for both the scholarships that you are exactly suited for as well as the ones you are *mostly* suited for.

The need for the Scholarship Résumé came from my awareness that the number of scholarships available is allegedly approaching three million awards per year. Some websites claim that there are over three million scholarships valued at over sixteen billion dollars in support available for

students just like you each year!

If you applied to only one-third of the scholarships that are available,

"I finally finished applying to all those scholarships!"

and if each application took fifteen minutes, it would take you around thirty years to apply to them all assuming you didn't sleep – ever.

So how do we approach such a large number of possible wins without working well past the point of diminishing returns?

How the Scholarship Résumé Helps

When you put the work up front into building your scholarship résumé, you enhance your chances of being awarded a scholarship because of several factors. Once it is built, you can apply for scholarships more quickly. I was talking with one parent who was frustrated and had given up on helping her son apply for two scholarships. Yes, given up. She had been entering the data required via a particular scholarship's website. It took time to find the information the application required, then she had to enter it all in, which again took time. As she submitted the application, she received a notice that the information had been lost! "Please re-enter the data," was all the support the site offered. Frustrated with that scholarship application site, she moved to a second site and after a couple of hours of striving to accurately enter the information on this one, the same thing happened! She told me that it was "easier to pay full tuition" than to frustrate her life with futile efforts. While that may have been an option for her, it's a fiscally foolish one when you consider how quickly the information could be entered from her scholarship résumé and what the potential payoffs could be.

Having all of your information prepared and at your fingertips will help you speed the scholarship application process, and if the system loses your information, entering it again will not be an arduous undertaking. Not everyone has the option to pay full tuition, but everyone has limited time. Your scholarship résumé will save you time and spare you similar frustrations.

Another way the Scholarship Résumé can help you is by focusing your application efforts. Just like I wouldn't try to create a résumé to apply for a nursing position (seeing blood makes me faint), you can focus your efforts on refining your scholarship résumé to provide the best opportunity to win the awards that match your skills, background, or interests. Within this book, I have included links to several free downloadable worksheets. Some of these will help you not only build your personalized scholarship résumé, but they will also guide you to the scholarship areas you should be focusing on.

Once you have your focuses identified, you'll recognize another way your scholarship résumé can help – multiple application submissions. This is related to increasing the speed of the application process: it's the other side of that same coin. The Scholarship Résumé simplifies and streamlines the application process, which enables you to submit more applications. Think of it like this: assume you have to go dig a ditch along the side of your yard. As you are given this task, you are also allowed to select the tools you use to do the job. Looking up and down the street, you see your neighbors digging ditches with their shovels and they have been working all week long. Occasionally, a truck rolls by and some of the dirt piled up falls back into the ditch. Change just one element of this scenario: when you decide on the tool you use, instead of digging with a shovel, just like everyone else has always done and is doing – you go for the backhoe! Yes! You can accomplish in one hour what everyone else has taken all week to do! The Scholarship Résumé is your backhoe to streamlining the scholarship application process.

The final benefit of the Scholarship Résumé is that it organizes your information. When you are applying for scholarships, there is often information from various sources required (personal data, school data, extracurricular experiences, etc.) and when you have it *all* at your fingertips, you will be better prepared and more efficient in sharing that information as part of your application.

SCHOLARSHIP RÉSUMÉ BENEFITS

1. Speeds the Application Process

2. Focuses Application Efforts

3. Simplifies Submissions

4. Organizes Information

Who Can Use the Scholarship Résumé?

While the Scholarship Résumé was originally developed for those in high school, it can be used by parents trying to help their students, as well as college students who are already in university. Once you have accumulated a history of activities, it's easy to forget crucial pieces of information

– this is true whether in high school or college. There are many scholarships that are available to either college students or high school students as well as those that either group is ineligible for.

When I have done informal surveys of how many scholarships an incoming college student has applied for, the answer is usually "between three and five" or somewhere in the single digit range. When I ask college students how many scholarships *they* had applied for while in college, the answer in 99% of the cases is ZERO! It is not a matter of who **can** use the Scholarship Résumé, but why everyone **should** use it!

When and How Should I Start?

The best place and time to start is here and now. I used to get excited about a new skill or activity I was planning to undertake and would think to myself, "I can start that on Monday, since it's the beginning of the week," or worse, at the beginning of the month or year! Start now – today – this minute. By reading this book, you have already begun! Congratulations!

Beyond reading this book, the next step will involve finding a safe place to put all of the information you collect. I highly recommend a digital media source that you regularly back up. There are many free sources like *DropBox, iCloud,* and *Amazon Cloud Drive* that can provide you with a great place to store your information. Then it becomes a matter of capturing the information as it occurs. It's important to remember to frequently do this, so consider setting reminders to keep your information current. I will confess that many people find that this is the most critical step, and the most difficult. As famous motivational speaker Jim Rohn said, "What is easy to do, is also easy not to do." In order to try to help you be successful in this step, I have created the Scholarship Résumé Repository which is available as part of the Full Ride Scholarship Program we've built to help you be even more successful in winning scholarships and eliminating college costs.

Since so many struggle with the follow-through of even the things that are good for them, I created this program that will figuratively drag you through to completion. The *Full Ride Scholarship Program* (*www.scholarshipkeys.com/fullride*) does have a fee associated with it, but if you follow the program, I guarantee that you will eliminate at least $1,000 off your college costs, or I refund your money! My goal is to help everyone be successful at the techniques that are outlined in this book. (Note: There are many other benefits to joining the Full Ride Scholarship Program. The Scholarship Résumé shows you one, but there are several other ways to get free money for college beyond scholarships that are wrapped up in this same program.) The information that you will learn in this book will allow you to be more successful in pursuit of receiving scholarship dollars; the Full Ride Scholarship Program provide additional benefits and opportunities for those who are interested.

Now that you have a basic understanding of what the Scholarship Résumé is, let's investigate the specific elements of the Scholarship Résumé.

CHAPTER 2:
THE ELEMENTS OF
THE SCHOLARSHIP
RÉSUMÉ

This overview will help you see how all the components of the Scholarship Résumé work together to ensure your success, regardless of the various nuances of each scholarship application.

Chapter 2: The Elements of the Scholarship Résumé

Just like a typical job résumé is made up of standard sections, I have taken those sections and drawn parallels to the scholarship application process and developed similar sections in the Scholarship Résumé.

At the top of every résumé is your personal information: name, address, contact information, etc. Your PERSONAL INFORMATION is also required for your scholarship résumé. This information will be covered in greater detail in Chapter 3, but in your scholarship résumé the personal information will get quite personal indeed. Some scholarships, especially grant applications and financial aid applications for the federal government, will require personal and specific information on the student and his/her parents, including bank balances, assets, and ethnicity, among other things - think tax information for the entire family.

The next segment of the Scholarship Résumé is parallel to the objective statement of a traditional résumé, the scholarship **ESSAY**. Just like the objective statement is the headline that is specific for each job you might apply for, the scholarship essay is used to set you apart and must be customized for each application. We will share in Chapter 4 how to not only craft a great scholarship essay, but be able to do it quickly for each application, so you can be more efficient with your applications.

The education section of your employment résumé corresponds nicely to your **ACADEMICS** in the Scholarship Résumé. In Chapter 5, we will share the importance of maintaining good grades as well as various strategies for doing so. While not all scholarships require a great grade point average (GPA) to qualify, there will certainly be more scholarships open and available to those with a higher GPA than those who are limiting their options by not earning decent grades. Fear not - there are ways to improve your grades if they are from stellar (or worse!)

The work experience of a traditional résumé is mirrored by the **JOBS, SERVICE AND EXTRACURRICULAR ACTIVITIES** in the Scholarship Résumé. When I interviewed job candidates, their scores on tests or in their classes was interesting, but was nowhere near as valuable as their work experience. Similarly, GPAs are important, but showing the other things that you have done is key. In Chapter 6, we will share ideas about how to advance these areas of your life and how doing this will provide advantages in winning those extra scholarship dollars.

Toward the end of most résumés there is frequently a section listing honors and awards. Often a résumé will also provide a place to list certain skills one might have, such as speaking a foreign language or some other talent relevant to the application being applied for. In the Scholarship Résumé, we call this section **AWARDS & TALENTS**. In Chapter 7 of this book, we share what you should do with your awards, how to keep track of them, and even how to seek them out, so you have more to talk about when applying for those scholarships. Many of you will be surprised at how many awards you may have won, and how with a little inquiry, you can get the documentation to support the awards you're describing. People like to back a winner, and when you show that you are an award winner, it reassures committees that their decision to give you their scholarship was merited.

At the end of your employment résumé and often on your job application, a number of references must be provided. This is exactly the same in the Scholarship Résumé – **REFERENCES** is the final section. In Chapter 8, we will share how you can develop and cultivate great references to

PARTS OF THE SCHOLARSHIP RÉSUMÉ

- Basic Background
- Essay
- Academics
- Jobs, Service & Extracurricular
- Talents & Awards
- References

provide not only for your scholarship applications, but for your school applications as well. The skill of cultivating references is one that is worth your time to develop, as your network and connections, especially those that know and believe in you, will be a critical component to your success in future endeavors. In fact, if properly maintained, these references and ones you continue to develop in life will likely help you get jobs, open opportunities, and provide even further networking connections.

Finally, in chapter 9, we will summarize many of the activities that you can do to ensure that you will be able to **WIN MORE SCHOLARSHIPS**. We share stories of things that have worked for others, and examples and routines that will lead you to success. This chapter shows you the power and advantage that you will wield once you have your scholarship résumé assembled. And just so you can review all of the various tables and downloads simply, we have added an appendix that has the images and links of the various free downloads that are available to you, so you don't have to move away from the book in order to see these valuable tools.

Pulling all of these parts together can be time consuming, but once the Scholarship Résumé is complete, it will serve as an invaluable tool in optimizing the number of scholarships you can accurately apply for on a daily basis.

When I was trying to teach the value of organization and planning in the workplace when I worked for a large audio electronics company several years ago, I used a video called "The Four Hour House[i]." The video was about an experiment to determine if the task of building a fully formed home, including laying the foundation, completing the landscaping, and everything else, could be accomplished in four hours. The builders began a rigorous planning session to ensure everything was ready and exactly right, as they would be competing against another team with exactly the same objective. The planning took weeks, but when all was said and done, the winning team completed the house in under the four hours of allotted time.

The same principle applies when using the techniques taught in this book. When you properly plan and build your scholarship résumé, it will allow you to apply to many scholarships per day, just like the home builders were able to execute building the home in record time. Take the time to refine your scholarship résumé – it could be worth thousands of dollars throughout your college years!

DR. JOHN W. MITCHELL

CHAPTER 3: YOUR PERSONAL 411

Each scholarship application will require information about you. For the most part, this is very straight-forward information that you already possess. That being said, there are parts of your life and background that, if well considered, will open additional scholarship and grant opportunities to you that might otherwise be missed.

Chapter 3: Your Personal 411

Many of us have a richer background than what we typically consider. In my case, I never took advantage of the fact that my father was a veteran (there are scholarships for that) or the fact that my great-uncle was a Native American chief (there are grants for that). The more connections and discoveries about your background you can make, the more scholarships that you can apply for. Your personal information or Basic Background portion of the

Scholarship Résumé is one way to better understand what additional awards you might be eligible for and one of the easiest sections of your scholarship résumé to complete. This is primarily due to the fact that seventy-five percent of this information required you can just write down off the top of your head – right now. Let's review exactly what kind of information you should make sure you have immediate access to.

Personal Information

The personal information that will be required for your scholarship résumé starts with your legal name. Make sure when you submit your applications for scholarships (this goes for college applications as well if you are not already enrolled) that you use your full legal name – the one on your birth certificate, passport, or government identification. If you use a nickname or shortened name you run the risk of not receiving the award that you win - it might be sent to the wrong person. In cases where the award is handled directly with the university, it could be refused or, in the most extreme cases, be denied to you on the grounds of providing false information (extremely unlikely, but why generate the hassle? – just use your legal name).

Additionally, you should have your Social Security number at hand. While many years ago it was common practice for you to have to provide your Social Security number up front, it is typically required now only if you win a direct distribution award. The awarding institution will use it to fill out the proper tax forms for the award. Declining to provide your Social Security number will likely nullify your award. **CAUTION**: think twice (or even three or four times) about providing your Social Security number prior to winning an award. It is just good practice *not* to share your Social Security number unnecessarily. If an application requires it, and you are really sure it is legitimate, I would still call the awarding body and request why they need that information prior to the award.

Let me simplify this even further – do **NOT** give out your Social Security Number when applying.

Other data required under this personal information heading may include your address, parents' names and addresses, e-mail address, and other ways for the committee to contact you should you win.

Financial

The next set of information that you will need to have on hand is financially related. For government awards and consideration, you will be required to provide your most recent tax return information. If you are a minor or covered by your parents' tax returns, their information will likely be required as well. Most of the information of a financial nature will be submitted via the Fast Application for Federal Student Aid (FAFSA) and via the university you are attending, should you desire some aid packages from the institution itself. Again, providing official documents to a scholarship group regarding your finances is a warning sign – think many times before doing so, and

Security Tip

When you are applying for scholarships, consider using *a separate e-mail for your applications*. It is not unusual for some scholarship companies to sell their applicants list (they should at least be letting you know if they do this in their disclaimers section). If you want to avoid the additional spam, sign up for a free gmail.com or yahoo.com e-mail account and then use that account for the purposes of reviewing updates on your scholarships.

then don't. If they require confirmation of your eligibility for needs-based awards, most organizations will likely ask permission to approach your school's financial aid office for their approval.

On the FAFSA front, the kind of information required will include[ii]:

- ❖ Name of student and parents
- ❖ Primary residence address
- ❖ Federal income tax returns, W-2s, records of any other money earned (student AND parents)
- ❖ Social Security Number
- ❖ Alien Registration Number (if not a U.S. citizen)
- ❖ Driver's license number (if you have one)
- ❖ Bank statements and records of investments (if applicable)
- ❖ Records of untaxed income (if applicable)
- ❖ List of schools you are interested in attending
- ❖ An FSA ID to sign electronically

More in depth explanatory information can be found on the FAFSA website (**fafsa.ed.gov).**

Military

Another category of information you will want to gather is related to military service in your family. I wish I had known about this one when I was applying for and enrolled in college. My father served in the Air Force and even though I did not, there were likely some benefits and scholarships that might have been mine if I would have applied for them. Bummer for me – but you can learn from my mistake.

You, the student, may have never served in the armed forces (if you did and exited honorably, you are likely eligible for some major college support from the US government), but if one or both of your parents served, then you may also be eligible some sort of support. Even without additional support from the parents' service, there are scholarships and awards that focus on exactly that category. There are even awards for the grandchildren of those who have served.

By understanding the background your relatives may have in the armed services, you will better understand if additional categories of scholarships and awards are open to you.

Ethnicity

Your individual ethnicity is also important. Most universities believe that working with a diverse group tends to provide a better learning environment. I experienced this during my MBA studies. Our executive program group of students or *cohort* was made up of twenty-four students. In our cohort, we were split down the middle with basically an equal number of men and women. Additionally, we represented diverse countries across the major continents (North America, Europe, and Asia). Beyond that, our educational and career backgrounds provided even further diversity (engineering, business, finance, sales, marketing, information technology, etc.) across a wide scope of industries (medical, aerospace, automotive, computer, retail, property, and more). When a diverse group tackles a problem, there is a great deal of new knowledge shared and gained by all involved.

Universities like diversity because it seems to promote stronger learning environments and outcomes. Another reason

Diversity Resource

If you are interested how diversity can improve finding a solution, try reading *The Wisdom of Crowds* by James Surowiecki.

Even the opening experience in the first few pages helps illustrate how beneficial diversity can be to finding solutions to problems that face us.

for you to look at your ethnicity and identify any and all groups that you might fall into is that there are scholarships, awards, and grants that are specifically focused on a particular group, and by knowing that you can open up more scholarship application opportunities for yourself!

Make sure you have supporting evidence for whichever ethnicity you claim on your application. It is fully within the rights of the awarding group to request a particular type of proof of the ethnicity you have claimed on your application.

Religious and Community Groups

This last segment of information for you to gather involves your membership in religious and community groups. Many different churches or religions have specific scholarships that you can be eligible to win, so you will want to make sure you know what those are and look for their application sites. Another set of membership awards that you should be aware of include local community service groups like Kiwanis, Rotary, or Lions clubs, as each of these may have local scholarships and certainly have regional or national level scholarships you can apply for.

Recently, I met a woman who is the former president of her local Rotary Club, and she shared with me that there were several scholarship awards that didn't go to *anybody* because nobody applied. Think of that! Just by applying, some students could have received those cash awards! Their families didn't even have to be members of the Rotary Club. Those experiences will hopefully be rarer as time goes on, but you need to apply to all of them – especially if your family is already a member.

Generic clubs or membership listing should also be included as well. If your family has a membership at a golf course, country club, boys or girls club, YM/WCA - just about anything - list it. It's an opportunity for you to find out if they offer scholarships, and how you can apply for them as well.

Summary

Now that you have an understanding of what information you should have at your digital fingertips for the first part of your scholarship résumé (Basic Background), you need to actually go and gather that information. For those of you who like to work with printed materials, or who like to have downloaded sheets to review, I have provided you with a free list of the various things you should include in your Basic Background of your scholarship résumé at _www.scholarshipresume.com_.   (All of the free downloads from this book are located at that same address.)

DR. JOHN W. MITCHELL

CHAPTER 4: DECONSTRUCTING THE SCHOLARSHIP ESSAY

The pieces and strategies to creating a solid Scholarship Essay are discussed. Don'ts and Do's are shared as well as the best ideas on how to rapidly generate a great essay for each individual scholarship that you apply for. This is will be one section you will want to visit again once you have finished writing your scholarship essay.

Chapter 4: Deconstructing the Scholarship Essay

Not everyone is a great writer. I was actually in my junior year of high school before I finally "got it" with regard to exactly what a misplaced modifier or a run-on sentence was. It took a connection with a particularly wonderful teacher that was willing to be patient, fun, and to beat it into my head. Mrs. Randolph used to play music in the classroom while we wrote; taught us the "W's" of journalism; and, of course, helped me finally understand what those red marks on my papers meant. Believe me, other teachers were great, but I just didn't connect with

them. I enjoyed writing, but I did not enjoy making sure every last jot and tittle were correct with regard to my grammar.

It was an "ah-ha" moment for me when I finally realized that it was okay to ask for help, as long as the content was mine. That idea became even clearer when, as a finalist in a writing contest, some other students and I were able to visit with a published author. As the author came out to address us, he told us that we didn't need to worry too much about all this grammar stuff, as editors would clean up our copy for us. You could hear the groan of every English teacher in the room! We will talk about the importance of having someone else review your writing a little later on in this chapter.

There are many reasons for a scholarship essay to be included as a portion of your scholarship application. Much of the information that you share in your scholarship application (grades, classes, and activities) will paint a general picture of you, but the essay will help separate you from the masses. If well-constructed, your scholarship essay will help the scholarship committee see and understand exactly why you should be the person that receives the scholarship they are preparing to provide. If poorly constructed, you will allow the committee to easily add your name to the "denied" list and not look at your application again. There are several types of essay questions. Several of the most common essay questions are listed below in the call out box.

There are some basic areas that scholarship essays tend to cover.

Sample Essay Categories[iii]

- o   Your Field of Specialization and Academic Plans
- o   Current Events and Social Issues
- o   Personal Achievements
- o   Future Plans and Goals
- o   Financial Need and
- o   Random Topics

With the exception of the last one, you should think of stories and experiences that relate to each of these areas and then include them as you create your über-essay.

SOME COMMON SCHOLARSHIP QUESTIONS

1. Can you share a specific example of how you demonstrated a leadership quality?

2. Where do you see yourself five years after having graduated college?

3. What information do you want to share about yourself with the scholarship selection committee?

4. Who is your role model and why he/she is such?

5. What is your most meaningful academic project or experience?

Building Your Über-Essay

Because essay questions and themes can vary depending upon the scholarship you are applying for, it's difficult to provide advice that would apply to each one. However, there are usually common themes that are covered by these scholarship essay questions and, as you continue applying to scholarships, you will find that you can develop some standard responses to these themes. As mentioned above, it is important to get your drafts reviewed by a competent writer. This could be a parent, an English teacher, or someone else with great grammar and literary style. As it is important to have each of the essays you submit for scholarship applications be correct, it is vital that they each get checked.

What we want you to do is construct a single essay that works in all the stories, experiences, and responses that might relate to every one of the scholarship essay example questions you see above and any other questions you might encounter. Again, the purpose is two-fold. First, if you are planning to apply for scholarships every day (as I recommend strongly that you do), your English buff will get a bit tired of you coming to him every day for more editing. Secondly, when you encounter new questions that are similar to ones you've encountered before, you will already have proofed portions of the essay that you can readily include. You can pull these sections from your single über-essay and construct a customized essay that will knock the scholarship committee's socks off! Make sure the work is yours, but then break out parts of your essay and customized polished portions to piece together perfect responses to the question that you might be asked (like those in "Sample Essay Questions" shown above).

Top 10 Don'ts & Do's

The following is a list of my top ten don'ts and do's of scholarship essay writing. I've distilled this list from comments shared by various scholarship essay readers, advice columns, and other personal preferences that have been shared.

Top 10 Don'ts

1. **<u>Don't Have Misspellings or Grammar Errors</u>**: I don't claim to be the world's most correct writer, but you have to avoid these kinds of errors if at all possible. I took a modern English usage course from an editor in college and the first week he provided a thirty-four sentence quiz wherein the class was to identify the grammatical errors in each sentence. He informed us that in all the years of giving that quiz, no one, not once, had identified

them all correctly. Either they found non-existent "errors" or did not find the actual errors. Most self-proclaimed grammar "experts" really understand only three or four rules and focus on those types of mistakes. After you've written a draft, spell check, grammar check, and if possible, I highly recommend having an English proficient check what you have written. One last trick: many computers offer the capability to read your essay out loud – do this. This will help you hear awkward phrases that you might skim right over when you re-read in your head.

2. **<u>Don't Whine or Share Your Sob Story</u>**: I'm going to be a little harsh in this one, so buckle your seatbelts. I know you need the money, but honestly, every student applying for a scholarship feels he needs the money. As someone who has seen too many sob stories written into applications and talked with others who have read them as well, you would be wise to not share a "woe is me" story. If you are going to speak about your hardships - and they may very well be legitimate - the right way to go about it is to share how you *overcame* the hardship. Scholarship committees want to know that their funds are going to someone who will

succeed with the money they're awarding, not just wallow in misery when things go wrong.

3. **<u>Don't Forget the Question</u>**: You would be surprised how many essays provide just a cursory reference to the question in the first sentence and then do nothing to further the point. When an essay question asks you to answer something, make sure you respond to that question. If it asks you to demonstrate service, make sure you show with your words and stories exactly how you demonstrated service. If you don't answer the question – don't expect to win.

4. **<u>Don't Write Too Much</u>**: When an essay question provides a guideline to the length of the work that should be provided, follow those guidelines. If there are no guidelines offered, don't overdo it. It is rare that you will find an award-winning scholarship essay that is much longer than five paragraphs (unless a longer work is requested). In the members' section of the ***Full Ride Scholarship Program***, the winning essay samples that are included all fall within this five paragraph limitation. Many great writers over the centuries have shared the same thought which Benjamin Franklin penned, "*I have already made this paper too long, for which I must crave pardon, not having now*

time to make it shorter." Take the time to craft a shorter response.

5. <u>**Don't Talk Over Your Head**</u>: When you're writing, use your natural voice. If you're accustomed to using your SAT vocabulary, that's fine, but make sure you are not forcing it. Too often it is painfully evident that the author of an article has just located the thesaurus function in her word processor. Clarity with descriptive adjectives is what to shoot for. "While struggling with the conflict I was presented with, I found my mentor's words suddenly springing to mind – I knew the response that would allow both of us to move our goals forward!" is much better than, "While besieged by my antagonist's barney, my cognizance moseyed upon my advisor's libretti – I discerned the rejoinder that would afford a conjoint consequence!" This example segues nicely to the next point.

6. <u>**Don't Come Off as a Snob**</u>: Yes, you are trying to impress the reader of your essay, but don't do it by giving the impression of boastfulness. When I was much younger, an elderly gentleman came to our Sunday school class to teach us about humility. He told us that we should not lie or hide our accomplishments, but should bear witness of them in a factual manner. "If you were applying for a job

and were asked if you were good with computers, if you responded, 'No, not really,' in an attempt to be humble about your talents – you would not get the job," he explained. If you are good at something, it's fine to state it, but that statement can be done in such a way that it does not come across as boastful.

7. **Don't Use the Same Essay for Each Scholarship**: In my free *College Cost Reduction* seminar, I share ideas about how to write one essay for all your scholarship applications and then break it apart and customize it for each specific application. Remember the second part of this advice and don't use the same essay for everything. The advice I give is primarily for the benefit of those you are consulting with for proofing help. Themes might be the same, but take five minutes and give each particular essay a custom touch.

8. **Do NOT Steal**: There are various example essays available on the Internet. They are there to provide you with ideas and formatting examples, not as pieces to cut and paste and call your own. Detecting that kind of misappropriation is easier than ever: there are several software packages that can analyze your essay and spit out a nice report of how much of it is plagiarized. (Welcome to the digital world!) It is NOT worth it, even if you're

not caught. In this same vein, don't use cliché, trite or overused phrases such as: "in conclusion…" or "killing two birds with one stone." You'll receive no points for originality with any of these approaches.

9. **<u>Don't Give Your Life History</u>**: The essay will provide you an opportunity to share a screenshot of your life. Don't abuse this opportunity by sharing your whole life story. I know you are a wonderful person, and the committee probably suspects it, but they don't need to have their noses rubbed in it. One strong story that illustrates the point requested in the question will suffice.

10. **<u>Don't Be Too Opinionated or Offensive</u>**: As you don't know who the readers are, you must be careful not to go too far in your essay. Stay away from polarizing political bias that is not required specifically by the topic. Don't share insights that could be viewed as offensive or unnecessary – gross descriptions or explicitly sexual references are rarely found in a winning essay. Don't use profanity. If you feel this directive is stifling your creativity or freedom of expression – it is not. It *is* helping your essay to be considered.

Top 10 Do's

1. **Tell Your Story With a Story**: When you begin to share your thoughts on the given topic, make sure you tell a story. Stories are engaging and memorable. You still need to be succinct (see Don't Tip #4), but by sharing an experience that illustrates your point, you will emphasize your message in a memorable way. Think of any speaker you have heard. You often will not recall the bullet points that she is trying to get you to remember, but if she shares an interesting story, you remember that story and, in turn, that experience.

2. **Provide Vivid Descriptions**: Now that you are crafting stories to illustrate your most memorable and applicable experiences, you need to ensure that those stories come to life. The use of descriptive words and phrases is key to this tip. "I went to work and saved money," may be factual, but it isn't interesting. "Each day I would walk the two miles from school to the grocery store, where I worked in the produce section. To ensure I would save money, I had a separate account set up where the store would deposit seventy-five percent of my paycheck" provides a much more detailed explanation and engages your readers.

3. **Brainstorm Ideas**: There are some fairly common themes that are used for scholarship essay topics (I listed a few below). When you are trying to make sure you have the right kind of information available for your essay response, think on how the topic applies to your childhood experiences, hobbies you have, service organizations you have worked with, sporting events you have attended or participated in, special events you have planned or helped plan, clubs you have been a part of and the activities that were associated with those clubs, religious service, scouting experiences, teams you have been on, and so on. The idea is to capture as much as you can – you can edit and filter later. Here are some common topic questions to consider when you are making your über-essay. Take a moment and brainstorm on at least one of these.

- What will completing your degree mean to your career and future?

- Why should you be a recipient?

- Who has been the most influential person in your life?

- How have you demonstrated leadership skills in your life, work or school?

- What effect on your education would this scholarship have if you're selected?

- What are your educational and career goals?

4. **<u>Show What Makes You Unique</u>**: You need to stand out! There are sometimes hundreds of other applicants that are applying for a given scholarship. Find ways through your essay to ensure that the committee members see that you are unique. Combining the first three "Do" suggestions will help you achieve this. When you are creating your stories and brainstorming, think of what makes you unique – and then find a relevant way to work that into your essay.

5. **<u>Capture Their Attention</u>**: Include a word or phrase that will stand out. A curious or interesting turn of phrase will grab your reader's attention. Don't overdo this! Just once or twice, work in a clever word or quirky phrase. (Just make sure it's grammatically correct - see Don't Tip #1). Your reader will engage with your essay more deeply. Don't think this is a thesaurus suggestion – it isn't. But even the use of an unexpected phrase like the exclamation "Peanut Butter!" can catch a committee member's attention.

6. **Be Positive**: When you're sharing your insights and experiences, make sure you're upbeat. A scholarship application is not the forum for depressing a reader. You're trying to get the review committee to get excited about you, not send them to the therapist. Show how you are optimistic about the future. Demonstrate how you have proven you are able to overcome obstacles and beat the odds. Convince them you love life and are buoyed up by the limitless opportunities in front of you.

7. **Have a Focused Structure**: The basic essay structure should be followed: Introduction, Body, and Conclusion. But not all parts of the essay are created equal. Focus most of your attention on your introductory remarks. You need to grab the committee's attention, give them a reason to keep reading your essay, and let them know what you are going to tell them. Of next importance is the Conclusion. The conclusion should leave a lasting impression. Remind them in a different way of the points you made and the interesting experiences you shared in the body of the essay. Make sure you provide clear statements that reiterate your answers or responses to the topic. Finally, while the body of the essay is usually the longest section and contains the in-depth information you are conveying, some

readers will need their attention retained and refocused - all of the prior Do Tips will help you achieve this. Also, make sure when writing the body of your essay each paragraph relates back to the premise shared in the introduction.

8. **Lead Your Reader**: When you write, your prose needs to flow. Think of your piece as a stream flowing down a rocky path. Every section of your essay is unique, but each part should relate to the parts that have gone before. The stream is unique at a given point, but it would not be at that position without having flowed over the previous stones. Remember, if it is difficult to understand how a particular paragraph relates to the piece as a whole, it will damage your chances of making a positive impression. The whole trickling stream is made up of water – your theme, which must be consistent throughout.

9. **Be Your Passionate Self**: Having had the opportunity to interview thousands of candidates for jobs, the one question that I always try to ask is, "What are you passionate about?" When you share your thoughts or connection to your passion, your eyes light up, your voice pitch raises, you gesture more, and your listener cannot help but be engaged. When you understand your passions and can relate

them to a given topic that is presented, those same engaging attributes definitely need to come through in your writing.

10. **Perfect the Craft**: Many of the suggestions above will fall short if you just dump the ideas on paper and submit them. You must work to perfect the craft. I will term it the Four R's: Review, Rewrite, Rest, and Revise. Record or write your ideas and then begin to implement the Four R's:

- **Review** your essay for consistency with your outline, with the theme, and with your introduction.

- **Rewrite** where there is awkwardness, lack of clarity, or uninspired prose.

- **Rest** or to take a break from your piece. Come back to it in a day or two and then move on to the final step.

- **Revise** or fine tune what you have written and create your masterpiece. As I've mentioned, if you are not the greatest essay writer in the world, it IS perfectly acceptable to work with someone (a parent or relative, friend, or English teacher) to have them provide comments and editing suggestions. You must however, make sure the piece is yours and not someone else's work. Be aware that you may need to revise more than once.

(If you would like a copy of the above list of items that is formatted for printing, go to *www.scholarshipresume.com* and download a free copy from there.)

Fundamentals of a Good Essay

When thinking about constructing your essay, make sure you use the time-tested three-part formula for memorability in writing. First tell them what you are going to tell them – this is your introduction. Next, actually tell them – the body of your essay. And then, tell them what you told them – the conclusion. Writing is about communicating your message, so as shared in the Top Ten lists above, you want to provide a clear and engaging essay that answers the question asked. If you follow this three-part formula, you can be confident that your audience (the scholarship selection committee) will understand the point you are trying to make.

Essay Pet Peeve

One quick little pet peeve of mine: if the question is something like, "Why should this scholarship be awarded to you?" don't just restate the question as your opening. "The reason this scholarship should be given to me . . .," is a poor way to open your essay. Don't blatantly restate; instead, find a clever turn of phrase or integrated way to share that you are indeed answering the question posed.

In the introduction, they will be informed of what to expect when reading the body of your essay, so when you illustrate your point with examples and illustrations, the readers are already listening and looking for the points you told them would be coming when they read the introductory paragraph. While in the body, find several ways to convey your message. Again, a rule of three is often helpful. Provide three stories, experiences, or examples of the message (the answer to the question) you are trying to give. And finally, leave them with a taste for what you told them in the concluding paragraph or sentences.

Persuasive Words

Certain words can help you more strongly illustrate your point. By using them, you can convey meaning without having to directly say, "Hey look at me!" and draw attention to what you are trying to do. It's almost like subliminal advertising, but the subliminal portion of the message is in the additional meaning of the words, not some secret message flashing on a screen saying, "buy Coke."

When writing, choosing the correct word can make the difference between being persuasive and putting off someone.

Isn't it nice to know someone put together a list of words that help persuade for or against an issue? The following words were gathered and provided by the University of Maryland on their website under the heading of *Persuasive Words*[iv] which might be used to help persuade for or against a particular point you might be addressing:

How to Influence

One of my favorite books on the topic is called *The Power of Influence* by Robert Calidini. If you would like to better understand the science of influence, this is the book to start reading.

IN SUPPORT OF	IN SUPPORT AGAINST
Accurate	Aggravate
Advantage	Agony
Always/Never	Atrocious
Best	Confusing
Certain	Cruel
Confident	Damaging
Convenient	Disadvantages
Definitely	Displeased
Effective	Dreadful
Emphasize	Harmful
Expect	Harsh
Interesting	Horrible
Magnificent	Inconsiderate
Most	Inferior
Most Important	Irritate
Popular	Offend
Profitable	Ordeal
Should	Outrageousness
Strongly Recommend	Provoke
Superb	Repulsive
Superior	Severe
Tremendous	Shameful
Truly	Shocking
Trustworthy	Terrible
Workable	Unreliable
Worthwhile	Unstable

Summary

Now you have some of the basics on how to generate a great essay for your scholarship application. There are several examples that can be found and periodically we put some of our favorite samples on the **Full Ride Scholarship Program** in the member's section (*www.scholarshipkeys.com*). Remember to generate one large essay so as not to be too much of a burden on those who help edit what you have written. Once you have it perfected, you can slice and dice pieces of it for each particular application you will submit.

When you are writing your essay, be sure to work in stories that will demonstrate several different qualities (leadership, service, academic prowess or other skill). This will allow you to not only utilize the story for different scholarship applications, but when you do provide that story in your essay, the reviewer will get even more than they bargained for. If they are asking about leadership examples, and you give them one that also demonstrates service or a particular talent, that won't be lost on the reviewer and could help tilt the scale toward a win!

DR. JOHN W. MITCHELL

CHAPTER 5: 'A' IS FOR ACADEMICS

While not required for every scholarship, many scholarship applications want to make sure you are a good student. Following are many ideas on how to maintain a good academic record or repair a problem spot.

Chapter 5: 'A' is for Academics

When I was in high school, I had a fairly easy time with my classes, but didn't necessarily care too much about getting great grades. As a result, my grades were mediocre. I figured that as long as I did well on the college exams like the ACT or SAT, universities would recognize how wonderful I was and readily accept me to their programs.

One day nearly midway through my sophomore year in high school, I was talking with my best friend, Chris. Chris was always a great student and since his father was a professor at the local university, he was able to provide some insight that had not even occurred to me. Chris told me that it was all well and good to ace those entrance exams, but that those exams were only part of the criteria for getting into the school I wanted to go to – my grades in high school were another critical component. I know that I had probably heard this from parents and teachers before, but my attitude likely got in my way. It was only when a peer shared this with me did it actually sink in.

I know that I had probably heard this from parents and teachers before, but my attitude likely got in my way. It was only when a peer shared this with me did it actually sink in. Fortunately, I was able to focus for the next two and a half

years and pull my grade point average to a level that allowed me to make honors, but just barely. What I will share in this chapter will be various ways to improve your grades, so that you won't be forced to make the efforts I did to try to rescue them (although I'll share those suggestions in this chapter as well).

While having great grades is not mandatory for all scholarships, having good grades will definitely open more scholarship opportunities for you. And, the more opportunities available for you, the more chances to win money for college and eliminate some college costs. Let's consider what you can do to keep good grades or turn around potentially poor ones.

Getting Good Grades

There are several ways to help make sure you get good grades. Each of these methods listed could fill up a chapter of information on their own, but I'll limit it to just a few sentences on each.

Show Up to Class

Attendance is most likely mandatory in high school, but when you get to college you will need to make the decision to go to class or not. Want good grades? Go!

Actively Listen

During class the purpose is to glean the specific information you will need for the task at hand. Your goal is twofold: learn the material and understand how you will be evaluated. Listen to clearly understand both of these areas - not everything is listed in the course syllabus.

Take Notes

As you listen, reinforce what you hear by writing down those items that you deem most important to the lesson being shared. Some people try to write down everything that is being said. This will often cause you to miss something being said while you are writing about the previous item, so write enough that you will later know what you meant, and know that you'll come back to it.

Prepare for Class

Read the chapters assigned. Complete the homework due. Review what was covered the few days prior. When you are prepared, active listening and note-taking skills improve. This happens because it is easier to comprehend what you're familiar with than topics you are not.

Have a Partner

Studying with someone will allow you both to stay motivated, as well as to learn by hearing things in a different way. Study partners come in handy for nearly all of the suggestions made in this section. You will find that the two of you will increase your knowledge much more rapidly than by your studying alone. And it's usually more fun!

Review Notes

After each class and no later than each night, review the notes you have taken. Even better, rewrite them and fill in the blanks that you didn't have time to write as you were listening at the same time.

Multimodal Learning

You'll want to use as many senses as possible when reviewing or practicing material. Don't just read something in your head, read it aloud on occasion. Use both your ears and voice. Write it again as suggested above, making sure it becomes part of your tactile and kinesthetic memory. If possible, teach the concept to someone else. If no one is available at least pretend to teach it to yourself.

Visit Your Professor/Teacher

Most teachers or professors either have office hours or review sessions. Go to all the review sessions and strive to visit your professor about twice a month to discuss what you are learning and look for additional insight to the material.

Seek External Sources

Hearing things in different ways can often help solidify concepts in your head. Creating multiple synaptic pathways to the same information will help you better understand it. A great place for this is the library, the Internet, or other sources such as the Khan Academy (*www.khanacademy.com*). Be sure the information you're taking is from a credible source, or you will reinforce bad concepts.

Assignment Redo

Look at assignments that have been returned to you and either redo them (especially any areas you missed) or look for additional problems you can work on, so you can master the material. This is where a study partner can be helpful. Quiz each other on material that you both have received.

Recovery Strategies

My son was struggling in one of his classes. After some encouragement, he went back to the teacher to discuss his struggles. Most students having difficulty with a class never take this step. When my son showed this initiative and desire to complete the assignment and truly understand it, the instructor was able to find options for him to improve on not only his understanding, but on his grades as well. Teachers want to help you find a way! It's up to you to ask and make the effort.

Even though you may be a great student, most students will occasionally suffer through a setback in their grades at some point of their scholastic careers. This can be traumatic or just annoying, depending upon the disposition of the participants at the time this occurs. The range of setback can vary from performing poorly on a quiz to having not realized they are halfway done with the term and it looks like that hoped for 'B' might be closer to a 'D'! So what do you do? Following are five strategies for trying to recover your grade.

1. Take Ownership.

"A man can fail many times, but he isn't a failure until he begins to blame somebody else."

– John Burroughs, *American nature essayist*

The first strategy in recovering from a poor grade is to own it. Don't waste time blaming your teacher, parents or anyone else in your life for a poor grade. The grade is yours – accept it. Now that you have understood the grade is yours, you can begin to take the steps to figure out how to NOT have that kind of grade again. What should you have done to avoid this result? Make a list which might include: review the materials with classmates, double check with the professor to ensure understanding, list all homework required, etc. No one else is going to get the grade or the learning, so accept that it's up to you.

2. Engage in Positive Inner Dialogue.

"Success consists of going from failure to failure without loss of enthusiasm."

– Winston Churchill, *former British prime minister*

Stay positive! The best way to learn something is to fail. When asking students about the subject areas that they remember the best, it is those areas in which they initially failed. No one expects you to know everything the first day. If they did, there would be no reason for school.

When you fail or fall short of your expectations, recognize that this is a necessary step in the learning process, and better yet, it is likely that it's the very material that you are struggling with that will become a strength for you. View a poor performance as the very next step to your success! (Because it really is, if you will stick with it – even Churchill agrees.)

3. Understand the Material.

> *"We now accept the fact that learning is a lifelong process of keeping abreast of change. And the most pressing task is to teach people how to learn."*
>
> – Peter Drucker, *educator and consultant in business management*

Now that you're aware that you don't fully understand the material – it's time to learn it. Don't be satisfied that the exam or quiz is over and in the past – learn that material. Consider that you did poorly on this material and then think about what you could do to make sure you understand the material completely. Would you redo your homework assignments? Look for other resources outside of class that might present the material in a different way? How about work with classmates to see how they understand the material and if their way of looking at it might offer you a different insight? Don't give up on learning the material. Ask yourself how this material might be applied in your daily life, either now or in your future. Not only is it likely that the material will appear again later in your learning adventure, but the very fact that you will work to master the material will enable you to see how to master other new material you encounter in the future.

4. Communicate with your Teacher.

*"Communication - the human connection -
is the key to personal and career success."*

- Paul J. Meyer, author of multiple success books

When you have not performed well on an assignment, quiz or an exam, now more than ever it is important to communicate with your teacher. Let me let you in on a little secret. Every teacher I have ever met did not get into the business of teaching because he wanted his students to fail. Teachers teach because they want their students to learn. If you come to your teacher and open a conversation with, "How can I get rid of my bad grade?" you are sending the message that the grade, not the learning, is the most important thing to you. Instead, go to your teacher and state something like, "It's clear I didn't understand the material as well as I thought. I have tried (list what you have done from step 3 above), but would appreciate your help in better mastering the material," and then listen for her suggestions on what you might do. Additionally, I have found it VERY helpful to attend the study sessions or office hours that the professor provides on a regular basis. This demonstrates that you are committed to learning and helps solidify you in the teacher's mind as one who cares about his topic. If the first time you talk to your professor is when you have a problem, you will be fighting an uphill battle toward gaining leniency.

5. Ask for Options.

"Successful people ask better questions, and as a result, they get better answers."

- Tony Robbins, American author and self-help speaker

In this last step, you actually ask for options. Leaving this step for last is critical, as the previous four may have already provided ideas on what options might be available to you. However, if at the end of meeting with your instructor you are still unsure of how to recover your grade, ask if she can suggest a path to recovery from the poor grade.

Many teachers will provide extra credit, retakes, a drop grade, or several other options, but it is human nature to want to help those who are striving to succeed, not just expecting a do-over like a video game with no more effort than just pushing a button. Ask without expectation, but with hope. "Mrs. Wheeler, thank you for spending some time and helping me better understand the material. I wish

I would have taken this time prior to the quiz, but I feel confident that I could perform better now, so thank you." And as you are leaving the office, pause and turn to ask as if an afterthought, "Mrs. Wheeler, are there any options for recovering from this quiz I failed? A retake or make-up assignment I could do?" Now it is time to wait, and see what is offered. Whatever is given, be grateful for it. And if there are no options, thank your professor for even considering some.

We all have times when we fail – how we face failure determines who we become.

> *"Learning is the process of failing and striving again until we don't fail anymore."*
>
> – Dr. John W. Mitchell, *the guy who wrote* this *book*

While this fifth recovery strategy is a good one, don't rely on it to save your grade. It should only be used when appropriate. If you expect to be able to recover every grade and don't prepare sufficiently to succeed, you will find this strategy mostly ineffective and, in the long term, counterproductive.

Study Habits

There are many great reasons for developing study habits. These habits will help you be successful in at least two key goals: learning and improving your grades. By focusing on learning, you will find that the good grades will tend to come easier. If you focus only on the grades, studying can often become drudgery.

By learning and developing good habits, you will be able to study smart and not just study hard. Take the time now to improve your habits. If you wait until the time of the exam or assignment, you'll likely be too late.

Below is a brief outline of some of the more common thoughts on improving your study habits. These thoughts are grouped into a few categories for both ease of finding and allowing you to focus on a particular area if you so choose.

Study Habit Groupings

- Mindset
- Environment
- Communication
- Preparation

- Planning
- Techniques
- Health
- Learning Style

The complete list is available as a PDF download at *www.scholarshipresume.com* so you can print it out and post it in a convenient location as a reminder. Keep in mind there are nearly one hundred suggestions, (only twenty-four are listed below) so choose the ones that work for you.

Mindset

These are habits that are largely mental or emotional in nature.

- ❖ Approach with a positive outlook. Develop a love of working hard at learning.

- ❖ Avoid self-defeating thoughts like, "there's no way I'll get all of this" and replace them with little wins like, "I can get most of it done." Avoid the absolute in your internal thinking; give yourself a way to improve in your inner dialogue.

- ❖ Establish your values and stick with them.

Environment

Your overall study environment can have a significant impact on the effectiveness of your studying.

- ❖ Devote a specific area of the house or apartment for studying.

- ❖ Keep the study area organized.

- ❖ Only have things required for study near you when you study.

Communication

Occasionally it is necessary to seek the help of others. If you do not communicate your needs to others, you will miss out on connections, which will make this help increasingly difficult to find.

- ❖ Ask for help if you need help! This is OK! Make sure you know who to ask.

- ❖ Find a student or three in your class you can call on if you need help.

- ❖ Meet with your professor or teacher during office hours – form a relationship.

Preparation

The Boy Scouts have it right: Be Prepared. Proper preparation can help ensure the execution of your studies goes smoothly.

- ❖ Know your teacher's office hours.

❖ If your school offers a course on "success skills," take it. At worst, it will reinforce what you already know.

❖ Let your friends know when you plan to study and that you will be unavailable during that time. Ask them specifically not to call or text you during these times. Better yet, turn off your phone.

Planning

When you put off things until the last minute, your chances of success diminish. Here are a few ideas on building a plan, so you won't always be "cramming" at the last minute.

❖ Create a daily study schedule. Even if there is nothing due, keep the habit and either review notes or prepare for something due later.

❖ Create a "to do" list. Having a list of tasks written down will help make sure you can build them into your study plan.

❖ Don't lump all of your studying into one chunk of time. Regular intervals of review over time will help move the material into your long-term memory more effectively than a single massive review session. Take breaks.

Techniques

Here are some actions you can take to focus your efforts. Explore and see what fits best for you.

- ❖ Remove computers and Internet-connected devices when studying unless they are required for your subject.

- ❖ Don't take notes on a computer. It provides too many distractions and little tactical feedback.

- ❖ Work on the hardest assignment first.

Health

If you are not well in body, you'll find it hard to maintain optimal mental performance for your studies.

- ❖ Get at least six, preferably eight, hours of sleep per night. Your friends will be jealous of your solid night's sleep! The older we get the more we value our sleep.

- ❖ Balance your study and activity schedule. Don't do too much of any one thing at a time.

- ❖ Exercise at least three times a week.

Learning Style

The more you understand about how you learn, the more effective your studying will be.

- ❖ Get a learning style assessment done. (Many schools offer these for free - ask a guidance counselor.)

- ❖ Once you determine if you remember information better visually, audibly, kinesthetically, or however, support that style.

- ❖ Use at least one other style for variety in addition to your primary learning style. The more styles you use, the better you learn.

Remember, these are just a sampling of the study habit suggestions listed on the free download page at *www.scholarshipresume.com*. Download the full list today and start improving the way you study.

Transcripts

When applying for scholarships that require or are interested in your grades, you will often be asked to provide a transcript. There are two kinds of transcripts, official and unofficial. Usually, the unofficial will suffice for most scholarship applications. Unofficial transcripts can often be obtained the same day you ask for them at your school. When you go to request an unofficial transcript, find out if you are allowed to make copies. If you are not, request several. As you will learn in Chapter 9, you will need them.

If you do need to provide an official transcript, be aware that the processing of your request takes time, and often requires a fee. Plan to request an official transcript at least a week before you need to send one. It would be unfortunate if you made the request for the official transcript only to learn that processing your request will take you beyond the scholarship application deadline.

It's a good idea to review your transcripts after each term, and double check them for errors. Errors are much easier to fix if they are discovered soon after grades are issued. If you are a senior or fourth-year student and you find an error in your freshman or first-year grades, it is unlikely that you will be able to easily get that corrected.

Finally, understand from your school exactly how they calculate your grade point average. Most universities in the United States are expecting a 4.0 scale. My high school had a fifteen-point scale that was quite confusing, so it was important to know how that translated. Also, there are some "tricks" that high schools will play with your grade point average when you take accelerated or honors courses.

If such courses at your school have a special effect on your GPA, you need to understand exactly what they do when making the calculations. If your school does provide extra benefit for tougher courses, you will need to understand your raw GPA score as well, because some universities do not recognize an inflated grade regardless of the difficulty of the course taken.

Standardized Test Scores

Most universities require you to take a standardized entrance exam. Usually, it is the ACT or SAT. While this has been true for decades, some institutions have moved away from these standardized tests. There are some scholarships that will want specific section scores (e.g. ACT Mathematics score or SAT Writing section score), so it's important not only for your

getting accepted into college, but could also be important for winning some scholarship money to pay for college.

If you do poorly on one of these exams, it may be a good idea to retake it. If you do really poorly, a retake strategy can be most beneficial. Some studies have shown that the better you do on the exam, the more likely you are not going to improve with a retake. This same analysis showed that if you did poorly, it is more likely that you will improve your score from the first time. Juniors (or third-year high school students) who retake such an exam their senior year tend to see their scores improve as well.

The following are some success strategies that you might find useful in taking the SAT or ACT exams:

- Utilize an ACT/SAT study guide (Princeton Review, Kaplan or the like) for understanding the structure of the exam, what is being tested, and how you can best prepare.

- These same study guides will often provide practice exams – take them all.

- Review test information on these exams websites (*sat.collegeboard.org* or *www.act.org*)

- On-line practice exams are also available and will give you a good feel for the exam style (don't rely on the fact that a great score in a practice exam will mean the same on the real one). There are many sites that offer such practice exams - use Google to find the latest offerings.

- Specific course offerings are likely available in your area. These are costly, but can yield good results for you if you are diligent in following the exercises.

- Each exam is different. Take both the SAT and the ACT, as you may find that one better suits your test-taking style. If you perform better on one, then use that one for the applications you make to both universities and scholarships.

Advanced Placement and Honors Courses

There are many opinions about the benefits (or disadvantages) of taking an honors course or an advanced placement (AP) course. Ultimately, it will depend on the individual student as to whether this is a good strategy.

There are several things to consider when taking such courses. First, any form of advanced learning is a good thing. The point is the learning. The more you know both in depth and in breadth, the better prepared you will be to handle various challenges and questions presented to you in the future. Most honors courses and certainly AP courses provide additional depth of learning that should help you as you continue your academic career, but will also help you in your professional career. These courses often challenge you to delve deeper into a subject, so you can understand more fully the factors that both impact that field as well as possibilities of impacts on peripheral fields.

Next, as these courses are usually a bit more rigorous, you need to be sure that you are willing to put the time into being successful at them. When effort is expended to gain the most out of these courses, the return is usually equally great on several fronts. On the other hand, if your mental make-up or level of commitment is not up to the challenge of these courses, you would be better off not frustrating yourself and potentially lowering your grade point average.

Most often, however, the most successful students are those who are the busiest. Why is this? To maintain all the many activities that a busy student undertakes, organization and structure are an essential part of his life. When you are organized and focused on accomplishing all the things that you have undertaken (school, honors courses, sports, work, chores, etc.), you tend to be more judicious and efficient with your time and therefore more successful overall.

Finally, AP courses and honors courses do send a positive message to scholarship committees that are looking at your academics as a prerequisite for their award. But a 'C' in an honors course never looks as good as an 'A' in a regular course. If you have taken honors courses or AP courses and been successful, you will want to be sure to highlight these academic achievements as personal differentiators on your scholarship application.

A Few Last Suggestions

Similar to AP and honors courses, if you have taken college courses while in high school and earned college credit, these too are great things to highlight academic qualifications in your scholarship application. They demonstrate your ability to perform and be successful at that level, while finding a way to eliminate some of your college costs. Some schools offer concurrent enrollment and even have local colleges teach some of these courses in your high school. While this may not be quite as impressive as taking a class on your own, it's more impressive than a regular high school course.

If you are looking to be a better student, try the "T" sitting method. Imagine a capital T formed over the seats in your class with the top line of the T as the front row, and the down stroke being the center of the class. It has been shown that students who sit on the T tend to perform better in class. There are several reasons for this: you tend to pay attention if you are in those seats, it is easier to see and hear what is being taught, and you have better access to the instructor to ask questions without being overlooked.

Keep those grades as high as possible. If you don't end up with a 4.0, it's not the end of the world as there are many scholarships available. But the better you do, the more opportunities you will have to be successful in winning scholarships.

CHAPTER 6:
GETTING BUSY!
EXTRACURRICULAR ACTIVITIES, JOBS, AND SERVICE

Here you will discover the value of having a well-rounded Scholarship Résumé and how to develop it, even if you struggle to get involved.

Chapter 6: Getting Busy! Extracurricular Activities, Jobs, and Service

Have you ever wanted to get paid just to do nothing? Well, I learned from sad experience that there is nothing worse in the world. One of the first positions I held involved a project that was projected to take a year. We finished it in one month. We went over all the data, including "standard practices," with a fine-toothed comb over the next two months, and then there was nothing else to do. We were stranded in a remote location and had no real options. I was literally being paid to do nothing. The excitement of that lasted about two days, and then going to work and just sitting there began to drive me nuts. I remembered wondering as a student, *Wouldn't it be great if I could find a job that paid me good money and that didn't require me to do anything?* The fact is, getting paid to do nothing was actually no fun whatsoever.

In contrast to this early experience in my career, I have often found that when I get busy, I accomplish more. Surely you have met people who do a ton more than what seems to be humanly possible. How do they do it? What is their secret? There are several. One of my favorite quotes is, "If you want to get something done, find someone who is busy and assign it to them!" This works! Why? Busy people don't have time to waste on things that are unproductive. That doesn't mean they don't have fun, it means they don't waste time. The busier you get, the less likely you are to watch a superfluous television show or sniff out the latest bizarre video on YouTube. You just don't have time. When you are busy, you are forced to focus.

Early in my marriage, my wife wanted me to dedicate more time to her and the family. I wanted to as well, but felt that between school and work I just didn't have the time. So what did she do? She marked out every thirty minutes of the day for an entire week on a calendar. After plugging in all the necessities (sleep, eat, work, travel to/from, church, kids' activities, date night, school, and everything else we could imagine) we found that I still had 32 hours each week basically FREE! I had more than half a work week available to pursue whatever I wanted each week. This was a wakeup call for me. It is amazing how much time we spend doing inane things like watching TV, surfing the web, doing nothing, sleeping in, or watching a movie every week (or every day).

I highly recommend taking some time and trying this exercise. List every moment and every required activity. Color-coding activities such as necessities (eat, sleep, family, hygiene), productive (work, school, travel), desirable (hobbies, connecting with others), and wasteful or unnecessary (TV, movies, web surfing) can provide a visual representation of where you are and what those proportions ought to be in your life. Why am I pummeling you with this point? Because I am going to ask you to do more than you have in the past.

Get a Job

Why would we write about getting a job in a scholarship book? Because those who are gainfully employed hold a couple of advantages over those who are not. The first advantage that you have by being employed is that you are making money toward your college education. That one's obvious. As someone who is employed, you represent several things to scholarship committee members. First, you are, at some level, a self-starter. You have shown that you are willing to stake out your place in this world and be a contributing member of society, not just someone looking for a handout. Some committee members will see you as one who is willing to work for school, not just receive a handout for school. Another distinction you show when holding a job is your organizational skills. If you are working while in high school or college, it is very likely that you will be quite busy. Busy people who are also successful need to be organized. So you will subliminally send the message that you are organized by holding down a job. Lastly, and this was implied in the previous sentence, you will show that you are someone who is successful. It's good to back a winner, and scholarship committees like to know the funds they are awarding are going to a winner – someone who is going to be successful and productive with the funds they are awarded.

The kind of job you hold does not particularly matter. You could be a teaching assistant, fast-food drive-through operator, or tutor. The point is that you are a productive member of your community. Once you have your job, you need to look at what you're doing with Scholarship Résumé eyes. This will allow you to describe your work in terms that will relate to the kinds of scholarships you will be applying for. Look for the leadership and responsibility, initiative, reliability, dependability, etc., you provide while on the job. These are traits you will want to provide evidence for, and on-the-job, real-world experience is a powerful source.

Passion Worksheet

It can be difficult to decide exactly what you would like to do with your life. I was present for a lecture by eight-time New York Times bestselling author Robert Allen when he shared a worksheet he used to help others discover their areas of strength. With his permission, I have adapted it to help you discover the passions you might have. Once discovered, these passions will guide you as to activities you should engage in as well as scholarships to apply for. This exercise is available for free download at _www.scholarshipresume.com_.

My adapted worksheet is made up of four quadrants that are designed to stimulate your thinking and allow you to better understand exactly what you are passionate about.

Talents

List 10 or more things you are good at:

1. Piano
2. Basketball
3. Reading
4. Helping my friends
5. Solving problems
6.
7.

The first quadrant is titled "Talents."

In this quadrant you will list things that you are good at. Talents could include things like playing the piano, playing sports like basketball or lacrosse, reading, helping others, solving problems, teaching math, etc. Really, anything you are good at can be considered a talent for the purposes of this worksheet. The more you list, the better! Don't hold back on the things you list here. The list provided may only have slots for about ten items, but feel free to list as many as you want. This list will provide you a place to refer to for points to make about your capabilities in scholarship essays, ideas about which scholarships to apply for, and directions to take as you look for organizations to either join or create.

The next quadrant of the Passion Worksheet is titled "Beliefs."

Beliefs

Name 10 or more causes you'd fight for:
  1. Animal rights
  2. My grandmother
  3. Education for everyone
  4. My home team
  5. My religion
  6. Helping the homeless
  7.
  8.

In this quadrant, you will list causes or beliefs that you are willing to fight for. Things that might be found on this list might include animal rights, animal play areas, aging relatives, education or Internet access for a segment of society, your local team, your religion, an underserved or unprivileged group, and similar ideals. Remember, there are no wrong answers! Keep writing and don't get caught up in whether it's practical or not, just focus on whether it's a cause you would fight for, protest for, or petition for, and you will end up with a suitable list.

Just like the previous quadrant, don't feel like you have to finish once you have listed ten ideas. Challenge yourself to list fifty or more. No matter the difficulty or impracticality of the task, list it. I love the quote from the 2010 movie *Alice in Wonderland* with Johnny Depp. Alice brags that she is often able to believe six impossible things before breakfast! Don't let the impossibility of the task stop you from listing it here – you may find that the very act of writing it down will give you the motivation to help make your belief a reality.

Interests

List 10 or more things/activities that interest you:

1. Girls
2. Xbox 360 games
3. Fantasy books
4. Playing lacrosse
5. Dancing
6. Singing in a band
7. Comedies
8.

The third quadrant is titled "Interests."

The Interests quadrant is where you list things that you are interested in. This should be items that are different than your talents (things you are good at) and your beliefs (things you would fight for). This is a list of more casual interests that you wouldn't necessarily count as a talent, but even if you could, add it to only one list. Some examples of interests could include video games, free reading books, social interactions, dancing or singing, attending sporting events, etc. Really *anything* that frequently grabs your attention could be added here.

This quadrant will be (in my opinion) the easiest to complete and fill up reams of paper. The trick is to have a curious mind and ask questions. For example, suppose you are flying on a plane from Los Angeles to San Jose. Just looking around, here are some types of the questions that you might ask to help develop some of your interests.

- Berneuli's principle explains the lift of the wings, what were the circumstances that led Berneuli to get to this aeronautical principle?

- I have heard that the majority of a plane's fuel is burned during take-off. Is this true? What percentage is burned?

- How many times have those airbags actually deployed?

- Why don't the bags inflate when oxygen is flowing through the airbags?

- How does air cause the speed bump sensation or turbulence during a flight?

- When communicating between different aircraft, why are the turbulence patterns fairly consistent? Shouldn't they be gone as they move across the country?

- What are the advantages or disadvantages of a private jet over a commercial one?

- Are there new technologies to help improve reading speed and comprehension?

You could do this for ten minutes every day and then boil the most interesting ones up to the top of your list for action.

The final quadrant is titled "Dreams."

Dreams
What would better your town/world?

1. Cleaner gutters
2. Safe playgrounds
3. Free WiFi Access areas
4. Renovated old buildings
5. Homeless shelter
6. Mowed lawns
7. Better neighbor interactions
8.

When we consider the dreams we would like to achieve, it provides us with a long-term purpose that will help us continue until we reach a successful conclusion. These dreams are things that you would like to see achieved. If you are fascinated by architecture, you may have a dream to restore or renovate an old building to its former greatness. Write it down. If you were horrified by the death of a child drowning in his own pool, you may dream of a program where all children are taught to swim and survive if they were to fall into a pool. Write it down. Like ice cream? Perhaps you have a dream of opening an ice cream shop where kids can invent and create their own flavors. Write it down!

Try to capture at least ten of these dreams in the list. This section might be difficult for some of you, so let me offer one more suggestion that I have adapted from renowned author Neil Gaiman. Surrounded by hundreds of English students, he was asked to share his secrets to writing and writing fairly prolifically. He shared that there were three key steps for every writer to follow. The first was to write. Once you have started to write, the second was just as critical and it was to . . . write. And the third and most important key for a writer was, of course, to write.

Adapting Mr. Gaiman's suggestion, if you are struggling with coming up with ideas on what you are passionate about, just start writing down things you would like to see changed or done away with or improved in your world. You'll want to focus on a local change so you can take action locally first, on one or more of these items. Following are steps to do this.

When you take all four quadrants together – Talents, Beliefs, Interests, and Dreams - you have the formula for developing and describing your very distinct mission or goal. Take a favorite or two from each quadrant and combine them to create a unique vision of where you would like to make a difference both for your community and for you specifically. Once you have identified your unique passion, follow the flow chart in "Starting a New Venture" (a PDF is available and described in the next chapter) and create your personal venture that will not only help you fulfill your passion, but provide a great source for experiences and insights to help you win scholarships.

Get Involved in Service

When I worked with the world's largest university honor society, we offered many service scholarships that awarded thousands of dollars to students who had demonstrated exemplary service. These scholarships and others like them often have no grade or academic component to them at all. So if you've failed to keep that 4.0 for your GPA, don't worry, there **are still scholarship opportunities for you.**

Hearing the term *community service* can be off-putting in today's world, bringing to mind images of juvenile delinquents standing before a judge with their heads bowed awaiting a verdict *forcing* them to render hundreds of hours of community service. The community service we are talking about should not be associated with punishment for wrongdoing. Wouldn't it be nice if the notion of "community service" was something aspired to by the general population, and not thought of as a punishment? Service scholarships are one way to brighten that image.

How can you move forward with community service? You begin with a cause you care about. I have seen excellent service rendered in a myriad of ways: to local schools, graveyards, dogs, veterans, the homeless, local museums, and many others. The opportunities are as endless as the passions of those who render such service. The key is to pick some activity or cause that is not only important to some group in the community, but **an activity you care about** as well. Your passion for this cause will come through in your follow-through as well as your stick-to-it-tiveness. Starting something that is meaningful to others is important – following through and delivering on a cause you believe in is critical, regardless of the potential of winning a service scholarship.

How to Start a Service (ad)Venture

When you have decided on the activity you would like to make a difference in, you've accomplished the biggest and usually the most difficult step in the process. You then need to do some research and figure out not only what is required to make a difference, but what kind of resources it would require to **make that difference**. Will it take money, materials, manpower? What other organizations would be interested in supporting your efforts? Is there another organization that does this that you can work with, or is this something that you'll be starting from scratch? Once you know the goal, the obstacles, and the resources required, you have all the building blocks of a great execution plan.

One quick note - if you are thinking of starting an initiative from scratch, this is a *VERY POSITIVE* thing for winning scholarships, especially in the service scholarship realm. Starting an activity from the ground up shows scholarship selection committee members that not only do you believe in providing community service, but you are committed enough to take it through the often difficult and sometimes painful start-up process.

When you deliver results with your initiative, you demonstrate that not only do you provide service, but you also **exhibit leadership qualities** – all things that scholarship evaluation committees value very highly.

Where Do I Find These Service Scholarships?

Now that you have determined the area you desire to provide service in, you have found the resources, and performed the service, how does this translate into scholarships? You can find these scholarship opportunities at national scholarship sites, state and business locations, and even the local parent/teacher associations of your schools. At the collegiate honor society that I led, we offered service specific scholarships, too. Many options are available with just a little investigation.

Before rushing off to those places to find service scholarships, you should find a way to **make sure that the service you rendered gets documented.** If you have a local newspaper or website that might cover such activities, prepare a detailed description of what has been achieved and how it was done, and send it to them as an article for their newsletter or blog. With a little luck, they will post it or publish it and you can then use that article as your proof when applying to related scholarships.

There are many ways your service can enhance your applications. Finding the appropriate service scholarship is the first step, but don't settle for just one service application. Apply for many different service scholarships! Additionally, this act of service **can be referred to in just about any scholarship application** you might find. These kinds of activities are the differentiators that will help set you apart from other candidates.

Service Scholarships Summarized

Our world, community, and you as an individual need to find ways to give back to other people, activities, or areas and *community service* is a wonderful way to do this. The added benefit of **service scholarships** helping those who help others is one way the academic world attempts to show it values those who are contributors to society. Find a cause that speaks to you, and let the causes of others reward *you* with assistance in getting your college degree.

Service works for scholarships on many levels. First, the time and effort that you expend will help provide you with real world experiences that you can use in scholarship essays or interviews. Since there are scholarships that are exclusively devoted to service, the more service hours you give and the more service experience you have, the more likely you will win these kinds of scholarships. Let me share an example of a service activity that was not only participated in, but lead and directed by students. These activities not only made an impact on those being served, but on the students who put together these efforts as well. Additionally, the press attended and covered this event each year!

It is hard to imagine anyone not being familiar with the tragedy that surrounded the terrorist attacks against the United States on September 11th, 2001. The most famous target was the twin towers of the World Trade Center in New York City. After aircraft were crashed into these buildings and in the other locations as well, rescue workers and innocents in and around the buildings lost their lives. Truly the world mourned the senseless loss that was incurred during that crime against humanity.

This event affected everyone in different ways, but I would like to tell you how one high school student put together an effort to remember those brave souls who lost their lives in 9/11. This student decided to post a flag for each person who lost his life (2,996 people in total), and to do so in a public place. The initial location - the local high school front lawn - was vetoed, but the middle school across the street was very happy to provide their front lawn as the place to place the flags as the anniversary for 9/11 approached. The student worked with parents, clubs, churches and other students to make the logistics all come together.

They needed flags, a way to place them in the ground in a sturdy but easily removable way (they would need to be removed after September 11th), people to place them, and a way to get the word out. People rallied to help in the effort through donations of time and funds. A week or so prior to the date, the project was up and in the front of the middle school.

The community rallied and applauded the effort, so much so that the high school across the street came back to the student and requested that the effort be redone in their front lawn, where it has continued annually. Local politicians and diplomats came, and a presentation and solemn ceremony was held on the eve of the event in memory of those who lost their lives. The student was highlighted in the local press, the school newspaper, and was the topic of conversation around the town.

This event took about three weeks of planning and effort, although in subsequent years less time was needed as the materials were reusable. For his effort, this student became well-known in the community. PDFs of the event coverage were readily available, and letters of commendation were easily obtained. This act of passion turned into service made a difference in the community. It also made a difference in the scholarships that were won by this same student. That student passed the project down to siblings who similarly benefited, and now that they have all graduated, a local school club continues the effort each year.

Local service yields multiple benefits to all involved!

Find an Extracurricular Activity (or three!)

I have five children. I can't tell you how many times I have heard the complaint "I'm bored" from one of my kids. With today's access to the mind-numbing immediate gratification and video game world, it is no wonder. As annoying as this complaint may sound, it is actually a good sign because there is now an expressed desire to do *something*. It takes some discipline to both recognize this moment as an opportunity and, more importantly, to seize it.

When you find yourself with free time, this is the perfect moment to explore extracurricular activities. The most obvious one for students working on their scholarship résumé would be school extracurricular activities. It is likely that there are a number of clubs and organizations already available at your school; organized sports would be one of the most obvious ones. Depending on your location, this can include football, baseball, track, tennis, cross-country, lacrosse, wrestling, swimming, diving, soccer, basketball, softball, or volleyball. In addition to these somewhat popular options there are other more specialize or niche sports like Ultimate Frisbee. Recently, I received a tweet asking, "Are sports required to win scholarships?" For an athletic scholarship, yes, *definitely*. For most other scholarships, there is no particular advantage of sports over some other extracurricular.

In addition to physical sports as an avenue for extracurricular activity, there are other competitive groups such as chess, math, debate, Go, or other strategy-based games. There are also clubs or groups in the fine arts: drama, glee, various choral groups (concert, madrigal, men's/women's, a cappella, swing, etc.), various band groups (concert, jazz, small ensembles, etc.), as well as art itself. You might also consider several academic groups like the honors societies, history club, science club, writing club, reading groups, and the previously mentioned math club. One final category of extracurricular activities are the ones that I call the miscellaneous groups. Some of these are historical in nature like the Daughters of the American Revolution. Others have sprung up from current social issues like the Environmental Preservation club. Just about anything you can imagine can become a club and there are even more available at the collegiate level, not to mention the various fraternities and sororities that exist there.

The above is NOT an exhaustive list by any means; there are probably twice as many that I didn't list. If you are bored and looking for something to do, there are many options and *something* is likely to tickle your fancy. I would strongly recommend getting involved in two or three of them each year! When you try out several that appear on the surface to hold interest for you, you hedge your bets that you be able to find at least one or two that will appeal to you and you can get more deeply involved. The next year, try two or three new ones, and the ones that fan the flame of your passion can become the ones that you stay the most active in and strive to influence.

I listed so many of these options above to trigger your interest. What if something I listed isn't available at your school? PERFECT! You now have the opportunity to *start* a club or group at your school that you are interested in! Let me take a minute to share exactly how you might go about this.

Creating an Extracurricular Group

So you read the list above and realized that there is no chess club at your school, but you enjoy playing chess with many of your friends and think it might be fun to start a club.

The first thing you need to do is find out from the school exactly what is required to make this idea a reality. Prerequisites might include a sponsor from the faculty, a budget, a list of those who are willing to participate once the group is formed, a list of officers, as well as a description of why you would like to do this and the benefits to the school populace. Most of this can be put together in fewer than two hours with you and a friend or two.

School Clubs

One small note of caution here, some schools only allow new clubs or groups to be formed at certain times of the year. Ask questions and find out when, and if the deadline is past, you have two forward moving courses of action: you can begin now to compile all the necessary data, so it is ready to go once the next deadline arrives, or you can find out if there is any option for a special allowance

Once the proper documentation is presented to the school, it is just a matter of following the process through to its conclusion.

Let me share a little about how this process worked for me in high school. One of my best friends, Chris (yes, that same Chris), approached me at the beginning of our senior year in high school. He shared that he and I should go about trying to bring back intramural basketball as a way to leave our mark our last year at Macomb High. We set about the task. First, we got an appointment with the principal to better understand why intramural basketball had been cancelled in the first place. We also asked what the process was to bring it back. Through this interview, we learned that we would need to petition the district school board at one of the public meetings. The principal also shared that there were specific rules and regulations required to both apply for approval as well as reinstate intramural basketball. We obtained those rules and set about our task of fulfilling each requirement.

We learned that we needed to have a faculty sponsor as well as a faculty member to be present at the games themselves. We approached "Spidey" who was a member of the physical education faculty and he agreed. Task one – complete. Next we needed to have a written proposal describing what exactly was going to be done, who could participate, and when and where it might occur. This was done and we described a intramural basketball season followed by a tournament where the championship team would have a final game against the faculty to promote school spirit. Next a petition to be signed by those who were desirous for this to occur needed to be signed. I went to a small high school of just under 800 students. We circulated the petition and obtained over 200 student signatures.

Finally, it was time for our big meeting with the school board. We sat through the various business items until our turn to be heard came. We shared our proposal and the fact that according to the school board policies, the district had to provide the facility for this venture as long as we met all of the requirements described above. The school district leaders had a couple of questions. The one I remember specifically was regarding the petition. They asked if we believed that all 200+ students would actually participate in the intramural basketball program we had described. We confessed that it was unlikely, but we hoped at least half would participate with the others coming out to support the games. They approved our request! Additionally, since we made it a co-ed league we had over 180 students actually join teams and play! Amazing!

Nice story, Dr. Mitchell, but why should I care? Well, this experience of bringing back intramural basketball not only taught me about how to accomplish things, but it made for very real experiences I could share (as well as newspaper articles I could provide) as part of my scholarship applications. We were definitely not bored. In addition, we made a difference that was felt by our peers and the community. And that scholarship cash both Chris and I received from various sources was a great bonus.

One more idea on the extracurricular front. If, on the off chance, you didn't find *anything* that interested you in that list above, don't despair. There is still another approach for you.

It is likely that you have heard of the Harry Potter books written by J.K. Rowling. Within these books is a sport called quidditch. These books are about a wizard school and how these wizards are trained. You should keep that in mind or the basic description of quidditch I will offer won't make much sense. The game is played while flying on broom sticks. There are goals at either end of the arena through which balls are thrown to score. There is also a very fast flying ball that if captured will provide an automatic win for the team that does so. Given that premise, imagine my surprise when my daughter shared that there was a quidditch club at her high school! Now, I have not attended any of the meetings, but I am pretty sure the students are not flying around on broom sticks chasing balls through the air. My understanding is that these students all very much enjoy the books and formed a club to talk about the books and other related events together.

No matter what interests you have, you can find or even create a forum for your interest. If you do happen to create such a special interest group, you have not only been able to add this to your scholarship résumé, but you likely will have strong experiences to share in your scholarship essay as well as potentially a leadership position to add. (If you create the group, there is no reason why you shouldn't be the president or, at a very minimum, an officer.)

Summary

In this chapter, I have encouraged you to get busy! There are several ways to do this that will benefit your progress toward winning more scholarships and developing your scholarship résumé.

First, get a job. Being employed shares several important concepts with scholarship review boards. Among them are:

- You are a worker! You are not lazy.

- You are at least attempting to be self-reliant.

- You are a winner – and remember, the committee likes to back winners.

Discover your passion. Remember to use the Passion Worksheet and not limit yourself to only ten answers in each quadrant. After filling out each quadrant, pull your most interesting points from each and see if you can craft a new passion direction to get involved in or create. Doing these steps will provide the following benefits:

- You will find new areas to get involved in.

- You may decide to start a new movement in your area of interest.

- It will help you discover related scholarship applications to pursue.

Find a way to serve. This is possibly the most rewarding of the "get busy" areas:

- You are helping to further a cause that you care about.

- More importantly, you are making a difference in someone else's life.

- You feel good about doing the right thing, and feel positively for making a difference in the community around you and abroad.

- You open an entire scholarship application category.

Get involved in extracurricular activities. This helps provide content for the activities section of the scholarship application and will also provide:

- Stories and experiences to share in your scholarship essays

- Opportunities to highlight leadership positions held

- Diversity in your interests outside of academics.

Everything you get involved in can help and be viewed as a benefit in your scholarship application process. As long as you keep your mental scholarship filter engaged, you will see additional ways to describe the things that you do and the things that you are passionate about in terms that will relate to the application you are submitting.

Store It All!

At the beginning of this book, I shared that there are many activities that you may get involved in and if you do not track them and record them on your scholarship résumé, there is a very good chance that when it comes time for applying for that scholarship, you may miss or have forgotten a key activity or experience that might have made the difference. Don't let that happen to you. Either use the Scholarship Résumé Repository that I offer or a similar system of your own!

CHAPTER 7: AND THE OSCAR GOES TO . . .

When you win awards, it demonstrates that an external group has recognized your capabilities as being above the norm. These awards show scholarship review committees that you are the kind of person they should be giving awards to as well.

Chapter 7: And the Oscar Goes to . . .

As you are striving to win a scholarship, remember that the committee is very interested in backing a winner. In this chapter, our first goal is to open your eyes to all of the various awards and recognitions that you have and will receive as well as some suggestions on how to merit them. Our second goal is to explore in some detail how to create your own business venture to gain stronger recognition and awards.

What's So Important About Awards?

You will find that most of the applications you fill out will want to know about any special recognition or awards you have received. Since you already have started your list of awards as part of your scholarship résumé, this should be easy to report. Scholarship committees like to see other awards/recognitions that you have received for a variety of reasons.

The committee wants to make sure that the funds being awarded are going to a good and worthy cause. Awards and other recognition are empirical evidence that you are worthy. Similarly, the committee only gets a chance to know you through the things you have written and submitted in the application. By showing committee members that others, who presumably know you better, have found you deserving of receiving their awards, you reinforce that their choice of you is a good one. Lastly, when the awards shared are particularly relevant to the scholarship you are applying for, that level of assurance that the committee is making a good choice increases dramatically. For example, if your article for a local paper is selected as the "best investigative piece" for the year and you are applying for a journalism scholarship, this would reinforce their decision.

You may find that the last point shared might present a bit of a "which came first, the chicken or the egg" problem. "How will I be recognized if the people who are doing the recognizing are waiting to see if someone has already recognized me?" There is some truth to that, but there are awards and recognitions and there are *awards and recognitions*. Using the earlier example, instead of having written the "best investigative piece," suppose you were selected as the editor of your school newspaper. While not an award, this recognition promotes your journalism prowess and you will have broken the cycle and begun the pleasant spiral of success.

What Kinds of Awards?

To give you a feel for the kinds of awards you should be looking for, let me provide a few examples that you could adapt to your particular areas of interest. As shown above, awards can take several different forms.

The first form is the most obvious – actually winning a contest or challenge that causes you to receive the award or certificate. There are many examples of this, such as winning a team championship or placing well in a sporting event, or your debate team may have placed second at a city-wide or county-wide competition.

Another type of award comes from personal recognition. Being selected as the team captain, or elected to be the vice president of your club, or becoming the editor of your school paper, are all forms of attention-garnering awards that will promote your worth to the scholarship committee.

An often forgotten type of award is personal achievement. Did you make a particular team? That's an award. Were you first chair in the orchestra? That's an award, too. Were you selected for a higher level choir? Yes, that's an award as well. Did you make it past the regional science fair and onto the state science fair? Yup. That's an award you capture and share when applicable to the scholarship you are applying for.

How Does the Committee Know the Awards are Real?

There is some due diligence that occurs with particular awards or recognitions. For instance, if you claim you were selected for the honor roll, it is likely that as the field of applicants is narrowed, the committee will reach out to the awarding body to ensure that the claimed award or recognition was actually received. Much of this communication path is through an electronic format, so it takes a shorter time to verify and more verification can take place.

Additionally, as many of these awards are posted in notifications or news articles that are available on-line, the committee will search for proof of the particular claim that you have made.

There is not a problem for you to provide proof of your award - you'll have it in your scholarship résumé! Remember to make a PDF file of the proof when you win an award or are recognized for your accomplishments.

There are also other ways you can ensure you have your proof. If you were sent a letter or an e-mail that states what it was or why you were the recipient, commit it to a PDF. If you received no such notice, request one. If that is problematic, then you should ask for a link to where the winners are publicized. Most award presenters will provide you one or all of the communications described above.

Collecting all of these documents and storing them within the proper categories (many of these most frequently used categories are provided in the Scholarship Résumé Repository that is part of Scholarship Keys' ***Full Ride Scholarship Program***) will enable you to quickly and accurately retrieve them when you apply for each scholarship. When you save the PDF file, be sure to use an intelligent naming convention to assure that you will know what each PDF is intended for. That naming convention should include the primary award (V-Ball State Championship), the date (2016 or H.S. Freshman) and, if possible, the category of scholarship you think the award or recognition would be applicable to (Leadership, Sports, Music, Service, etc.). The file name might look something like this: *2018 Volleyball State Champ – Sports.Leadership.pdf.* If you use this kind of naming convention, you can very easily recognize and find relevant articles for the scholarships you are looking to win.

Creating Your Own Venture

One of the best ways to gain the awards or recognition you are trying to demonstrate is to build it yourself. There are only so many football team captains, first chair violinists, and school paper editors. That being said, there are an infinite number of ventures that you can establish, lead, and promote to show your expertise in any of these areas. These do not need to be limited in any way to the traditional kinds of areas I have just listed. Recall from Chapter 6 the example of the quidditch club; no matter what interests you have you can still find or even create a forum for your interest. If you do happen to create such a group, you have not only been able to add this to your scholarship résumé, but you likely will have strong experiences to share in your scholarship essay as well as potentially a leadership position to add. Remember, if you create the group, there is no reason why you shouldn't be the president of the club or at a very minimum an officer. This will open leadership scholarships in addition to the scholarship directly related to the venture you have started.

Many individuals struggle with understanding exactly what to do to establish their own venture. To help overcome this concern, we have created a PDF flow diagram (***Starting a New Venture***) that will walk you through exactly what you need to do to get such going. As the PDF is just one page, below we share some more explanatory notes expanding on the main segments of the flow diagram provided on-line.

You can download this free document and other materials by going to *www.scholarshipresume.com*.

Start with a Purpose & Passion

The diagram below is a clip of the PDF mentioned above. As you can see, the process should all start with a purpose and passion.

We begin the process by asking several questions to ascertain the exact purpose you are trying to accomplish.

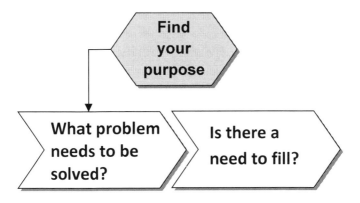

The first question to ask yourself is, **what is the problem that needs to be solved?** If there are dogs running wild and being injured on the busy streets in your area, this might be the problem you wish to solve. **Is there a need to be filled?** Is there is a group or organization that is already working on solving the problem you have identified? Is there a city organization (the dog pound) that might be working on this issue? Is there an organization that works on these kinds of problems (a local animal society)? Reach out to these places and find out what, if anything, they are doing to solve the problem you would like to see fixed. Even if there is a group that is claiming to be working on the issue, don't give up yet; you can still be the impetus to solving this challenge by working with this organization to help them better solve the issue they have already recognized, but obviously have not yet fully solved. Assuming there is a gap in the world that has left your problem unresolved, continue to the next question.

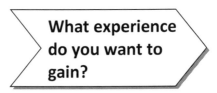

What experience do you want to gain?

Next, consider **what experience are you hoping to gain through this effort?** There are many answers that are possible to this question and they all depend on you. Maybe you want to solve the issue, or maybe you want to improve your scholarship résumé. Or there may be other or combinations of reasons. I would strongly encourage you to be completely honest with yourself as to why you are pursing this venture. The more clearly you know what you are hoping to gain from this experience, the more likely you will be satisfied with the efforts you are about to undertake.

You should also answer the question: **how would the world be better because of what you are doing?** If you can capture the vision of how the world (big or small – global or local) will benefit from this effort you are imagining, you will be better positioned to excite others with your vision. By asking yourself to **examine all the things that you complain about,** you are really taking a look at what you would be passionate about changing in the world. If it bugs you enough to whine about it often, it must be important enough to warrant some of your time to fix the issue.

And of course once you do, you will know that at least you will be happier because of the change you have effected.

While you are reviewing these questions, you should write down all the various thoughts and ideas that come to mind. Don't filter. Use this as a brainstorming session and you will likely find that you are able to capture dozens of ideas that will be important, impactful, and interesting to you. I would review these five questions at least three times, so you can be sure that you have many different potential directions to review.

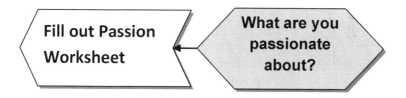

The next step is to look at what you are passionate about. For this we have the Passion Worksheet. This was described in Chapter 6 and you should review your notes from filling out this worksheet and combine the efforts with the answers to the purpose driven five questions we have just reviewed above. Once you have done this, capture your venture idea(s). Don't feel like you have to limit yourself to just one, you can have several. Initially you will focus on just one, so you can be sure to make some progress.

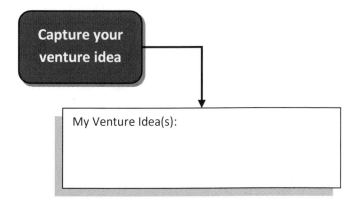

Do Your Research

The next step in the Venture creation process is to do some research.

In this stage of creating your venture you will need to gather facts. The best way is to start by writing down everything you know. Don't hesitate to include questions of things that you are pretty sure you would like to know or should know, but don't at this current moment. Include the little things as well as the big things. Where you have seen the issue occur? How often? Capture as much detail as you can. When you do this, you will likely surprise yourself with how much knowledge you have.

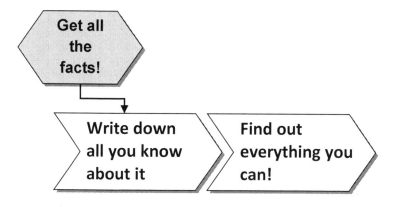

The next step is the real research area. Find the answers to all those questions. Talk to people who are near to the issue you are pursuing. Look up books or websites or blogs that might be discussing the issue. You may find that someone else half-way across the country is already doing what you are interested in doing. This is GREAT NEWS! Especially if they are doing a good job. Now you have a resource to help you do the same thing. Don't run away from an idea just because someone else is interested in doing the same thing. Keep looking to find out everything you can about what might be the cause of the issue, what previously attempted solutions have been tried, etc. If someone has already tried to approach solving the venture with the same approach you are thinking of using and they were unsuccessful – don't let this discourage you yet. It could be that the person or group that tried it earlier might have lacked leadership, funding, motivation, or any number of other potential reasons for failing. You need to examine these cases very carefully. Call the people involved. Find out what they did or didn't do. This can save you from going down the wrong path and wasting loads of time.

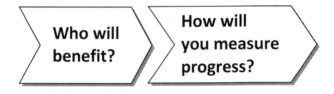

After doing your research and finding out everything you can, consider carefully who will benefit from the change you are about to undertake. The more people you can show will benefit, the more potential supporters you will have on your path to changing your part of the world. Figure out exactly how you will measure the progress you make in your efforts to right this wrong or overcome this issue. Without measures that will show progress, you risk the interpretation that nothing has been accomplished. Make sure there is at least one relevant measure, but preferably three or four. When you have multiple measures, you will have the opportunity to talk about the one you want (the one that shows the improvement).

Finally, make sure you have written down everything you have learned. Include with your notes the thoughts and concerns you had while doing your research. These will provide a nice dialogue to share on the other side of the equation – once you have accomplished your venture.

Build the Plan

Now that you have decided on your venture and have researched it, you are ready to build your plan to turn your idea into a reality!

To start your new venture, there are very likely a number of requirements that must be met. It is in your and your venture's best interest to clearly understand and fulfill all of these requirements. The following line of questioning will help you ensure that you have at least the basics of the requirements understood. As you go through this line of questioning, I would write out the answers as a checklist or a "to do" list, to ensure that no step is missed that could in some way come back to cause you problems down the road.

When you are looking at starting this new venture, you should first ask: Who needs to approve my endeavor? This could be the school district; a community; the local, state or federal government; or maybe a land owner. As you approach this individual or entity, you may find that there are additional approvals required that you were unaware of. Make sure you add these to your checklist, along with what is specifically required in order to gain that approval.

Once you fulfill these requirements, approval is practically a given. In addition to understanding the requirements, you

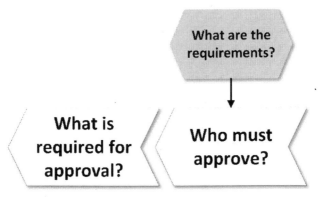

need to pay attention to any particular deadlines that you might be facing. To neglect to do so could jeopardize free funding or invalidate your application for another year. And, speaking of funding, you need to understand if there is any funding required. Some approval bodies will require some sort of funding to ensure a given request is valid.

Once you have made it through the understanding of the requirements phase of this project, it is time to really build a plan. In the figure above, I have highlighted some helpful tips for building your plan. The more detail you provide, the more obvious your next step. Don't get too caught up in creating the *perfect* plan before you get going, as you can continually revise your plan as you go. There is only so much you will know up front, so don't be afraid to follow Pareto's Law, or the 80/20 rule. What it basically means is that you can accomplish 80% of a task with the right 20% of effort, which is usually enough to determine the path you should follow.

Build a Plan:
- Start with the end in mind
- Work backward to the start
- Fill in the major milestones
- Add the minor steps required to achieve the major steps
- Adjust with deadlines

To build your plan, begin with the end in mind. Know the result you are striving to achieve and work backward from there. If you are trying to start a club at your school, design the club specifics and how it will be unique and make a difference. Then list what would need to occur for that to happen. Perhaps you will need to have one hundred people in the club to achieve the ends you are pursuing. To achieve that you might need to advertise. To do that you might need some funds. To get those you may need to contact all the people this venture will benefit to ask for support. When you make a request for funding, you might need to know exactly how much money it would take. To know how much money, you will need to . . . , etc. Work with the end in mind and follow the steps back to the beginning.

Next, capture the major milestones required to get you going. These could be: raise $500; establish organization; kick off first meeting; hold first event. Fill in all of the little steps required to achieve that milestone. Once you have done that, you need to order them. Does one of your minor steps or milestones depend upon the completion of another? Once you identify any dependencies, assign time estimates (how long will it take to do the task) and deadlines (when does the task need to be done by). And now you have a fairly robust plan to execute.

Once you have a detailed plan, it is easier to share your vision with others. If you are going for funding, it strengthens your position because potential fund providers will better understand where and how their monies will be used. This is critical for success.

Execution

The most important step in your venture is execution. If you don't *do* anything – it is as if you had never started at all.

Once you start, you may find that you have started a major undertaking and become overwhelmed. This is the time to involve a partner or a group to accomplish the project you have developed. As shared earlier, when trying to get the school district to bring back intramural basketball, it was a partnership that allowed us to succeed. Working together allows all to enjoy the success and, as an added bonus, use it in scholarship applications submitted. Finding people in your school or other social circles that feel the way you do about the issue is ideal. But that is not the only source of help available. Parents, relatives, friends of friends, significant others, really anyone who will put in a little time, will work at this stage. Obviously, if you team up at the earlier planning and formative stage, your team should be just as or close to as passionate as you are.

> **Execute your plan:**
> - Involve others
> - Get the word out
> - Keep a log of what is done
> - Publicize what you do!

The next step in successful execution is getting the word out. Some of the techniques and paths that you might use include: a school newspaper; a blog; a Facebook post; talking about it with friends; contests to generate interest; posters; and, if it is a not-for-profit event, you can possibly get some free radio time on a local channel. Use your imagination. If this is not your forte, this is another place that you can leverage a team mentality. Find someone who *is* good at the marketing aspects and get them involved. One of my favorite effectiveness quotes has been attributed to John Asseraff, who said, "Hire people who play at the things you work at."

Once you are underway, take a moment each week to document what is going on with your initiative. Capture the highs, the lows, and especially any press or coverage you may receive. This will be useful when you need to add stories or experiences to your scholarship (or college application) essays.

Priming the Pump

Finally, don't wait for others to discover what you are doing – actively advertise! This is a little different than the most of the marketing ideas listed above. Even without a budget to speak of, you can get some great press. The most obvious, but often neglected, idea is to invite the press to one of your activities. You can encourage this further by writing up a short blurb that they can turn into an article. If they don't attend, follow up with pictures and a full article to show the impact and save them some time writing. The real message here is, don't feel like you are at the mercy of the news or blog outlets to get noticed – bring your event, article, and cause to their space and make the job easy for them to cover.

Summary

There are several different techniques and ideas for promoting yourself as a winner in a class of your own. This way, you'll win on the terms that you not only dictate, but you are fiercely interested in as well.

- Winners like to back winners – show them you are a winner.

- There are several different ways to win – many awards you can pursue and demonstrate.

- Get the proof and PDF it.

- Build your own venture.

- Partnered ventures may be a good path – many hands make light work.

- Help the press cover what you are doing.

It is important to keep track of your awards as external evidence of your accomplishments and another's opinion of just how great you are. Remember to write the awards down, scan the articles where such things are published, or put them in your Scholarship Resume Repository as a member of the *Full Ride Scholarship Program.*

CHAPTER 8: WON'T YOU BE, PLEASE WON'T YOU BE, MY REFERENCE?

When references are required, if
you haven't developed them, it
is often too late to get a good
one. With proper effort and
attention, you can have some
great references to share with
your application.

Chapter 8: Won't You Be, Please Won't You Be, My Reference?

References. Who should you choose? How well do they need to know you? How soon should you notify them that you would like them to provide a reference? Can you use the same reference for multiple applications?

Why do scholarship committees require references? There is only so much that can be learned or gleaned from the information you provide in your scholarship application. They want a character reference at the very least. As members of the scholarship committee do not likely know you or what kind of person you are from just a few facts and an essay, they would like a corroborating witness or three. These witnesses should know you personally and should therefore be able to provide a more accurate picture of the kind of person you are via their responses to various questions or a reference letter. With so many scholarship applications, it is likely that you will want to make sure you have more than just two or three individuals that are ready and willing to provide you a reference when you need one.

Having solid reference sources who can speak knowledgeably about you and your accomplishments can be the difference between winning and losing a scholarship award. This chapter will share exactly how to solidify your sources and the references they will provide.

As you are likely aware, some scholarships (and nearly every college application) will ask you to provide references. How do you know the right reference for your application? Some of that depends upon the scholarship you are applying for. If you are applying for a math scholarship and provide a reference from scouting and from your English teacher, those might not be the most impressive choices. If their background is not obvious in its relevance to the scholarship's focus, make sure your reference clarifies their relevance as part of their submission (more on this later).

In this chapter, we will walk you through the reference development process and show you exactly how to cultivate and develop great sources that will be happy to provide you a reference because they know you, what you have done, and you make the process easy for them.

Who Makes a Good Reference?

There is a common misconception or myth regarding references. Many believe that if you can get a famous person to provide you a reference that you are a "sure thing" for winning the scholarship or gaining admittance. Some will spend extra time seeking out people of note and asking them to write a reference for them. Surprisingly, some of these folks will do exactly that. Because of their acquaintance with a parent or relative, when asked, this famous person will provide a reference for a largely unknown quantity – the applicant.

I strongly believe that this does not work well. While I may be intrigued by the famous person's writing of a reference, I am somewhat dubious as to their familiarity with the candidate, so even deeper scrutiny is invited.

A friend of mine had this exact thing happen to him. While the experience is based on a school application, the principle applies to all reference-related requests. I will share a little background on Donald Martin. Don worked at the both the Columbia and the University of Chicago graduate school admission departments. He reviewed thousands of applications at these two very prestigious schools. Each application required a letter of reference. He would marvel at the people that would provide these individuals reference letters. On one application, Vice President Al Gore had provided a reference letter recommending the student to the university. As the committee read the letter, it became clear that Mr. Gore did not know much about the applicant at all and as a result of the letter not clearly reflecting the applicant, that student was not admitted to the program.

Lesson learned? Good.

Let's get started on building and developing a great set of references for you! You can download the free Scholarship Keys Reference Worksheet at *www.scholarshipresume.com*. Let me walk you through it in the next few segments.

Building Your Reference Portfolio

To begin, build a list of potential references. For many of you, several names will come quickly to mind. Your boss, a counselor at school, a favorite teacher, or a coach are all good ideas, but let's examine why they make good reference candidates.

Build Your Prospect List
You should have at least 10 names to start

Good references will be asked to attest to certain qualities in the reference they submit, so when you are considering sources, make sure they have strong answers to these qualifying questions as well as they are a related and valuable opinion.

Most reference questionnaires will ask how long the source has known you. Although length of time is a factor, it is not a "longer is always better" kind of inquiry. It is more like a pass/fail. If your references all have only known you fewer than three months, that will be a red flag. However, if a particularly strong reference is short (less than one year) don't be afraid to include her. Just make sure that at least one other of your strong references has known you for well over a year.

The next question is typically in what capacity the source has known the applicant (you). This is where their background comes in to play. Some of the stronger types of references you should consider when building your list would be from some of the following areas:

- Teachers, advisors and coaches make good references because they have seen you in comparison to other students in your grade and in comparison to other students through the years.

- Clergy members make strong references as they are viewed as persons of integrity and when they speak highly of you, most committee members find they are trusting of the information provided.

- Mentors are good references. This is because they, too, fall into the teacher/coach category, and the fact that you have a mentor at all says you are forward-thinking and interested in improving yourself.

- Volunteer leaders like Boy or Girl Scouts or from a local charity also make good references as a general rule. This shows you have an achiever attitude as these groups focus on growing the individual and achieving goals.

- Employers make good references on a couple of levels. First, they know you and therefore provide a credible source of information, and secondly, they have valued your worth by paying for your services. Very few other of the types of references mentioned can state that they value you to the point that they pay you to maintain your relationship with them.

In general, your references should be persons of integrity. They should hold positions that clearly demonstrate their knowledge and expertise and should have either worked with you over a sufficient period of time or have worked with others with whom they can compare you. Remember the story about the vice president sending in a reference for someone he really didn't know that well. Don't let this happen to you.

Making Initial Contact

Now that you have created a good list of potential references, let's discuss how to start an engagement. Your

Make Initial Contact
- Meet face-to-face
- Remind them how they know you
- Establish rapport

goal of an initial contact is NOT to ask them to become a reference today. Your goal is to remind them who you are and establish rapport with them. If you have time constraints, you may have no other choice but to make a request, but if you can, find a few moments to do the following:

Meet Face-to-Face

Why face-to-face? The majority of communication that takes place is non-verbal. According to Dr. Albert Mehrabian's studies on nonverbal communication in *Silent Messages*[v], this number could be anywhere from 75% to the oft-quoted 93%. When you meet a potential reference face-to-face, you are better able to read his intent and interest in what you are proposing. Additionally, you have shown that you value him as you have taken the time and made the effort to physically go and visit him. If a personal visit is impossible, then a phone call is better than an e-mail. When proposing this meeting, make sure he understands that you are only requesting ten to twenty minutes of his time.

Remind Them How They Know You

If you are talking with a teacher or a leader of some organization, it is entirely possible that they may only have a vague recollection of who you are or have forgotten you entirely. Do not be offended by this. In my professional capacity at the world's largest collegiate honor society, I was able to get to know thousands of truly talented students. When some of them approached me for recommendations, I had to ask their patience with me and requested that they share some reminder of who or when we met. Be prepared to refresh your source's memory.

For example, when you make your initial contact begin with your name, and provide them a graceful out by recognizing that they work with many people and then share how they might remember you. Share the approximate date of your interaction with them. Also, if there was a particular event that would be help trigger their memory, share that as well.

Establish Rapport

This step may feel a bit like sales. It *is* a bit like sales. You are selling them a great product – YOU. When I was starting out as an engineer, I was concerned that my delivery of approaches appeared fake and insincere. I came to realize that people really like to work with, hang out with, and do things with those with whom they have developed some connection. The other reason for you to make an effort to develop rapport is that it might lead to a more dynamic reference when the time comes.

How do you make the connection? Be completely sincere. When you see parts of their lives that you can relate to or aspire to, share that factual feeling. Don't force something that isn't there. We humans have a sense for when someone is just feeding us a line. What are the kinds of ways that you can establish rapport?

- Make direct eye contact, but don't enter into a staring contest.

- Reflect the sitting position or hands position of the person you are speaking with.

- Talk about them more than about you (this might be a little hard in this situation, but try).

- Smile.

- Do your research. Know about them and their company and talk about what you have learned and which aspects appeal to you.

- Ask questions. These should be about them and their organization.

- Practice the active listening skills of: reflecting their words, provide positive reinforcement, remembering what they have shared, etc.

DR. JOHN W. MITCHELL

One last skill for developing rapport is fulfilling your commitments. Honor the commitments you make. If you say you will be at their office to meet at 10:15 am, don't show up at 10:18 am. One good way to be sure you fulfill your commitments is to review what you have committed to do at the end of your meeting. This provides a clear expectation, it makes sure you have shared what you are going to do, and it provides an opportunity for them to add or remind you of something that you may have stated but forgotten to list.

The Right Connection Path

While you are at your first meeting with your potential contact, share with them that you would like to keep them up-to-date on your accomplishments periodically in a way

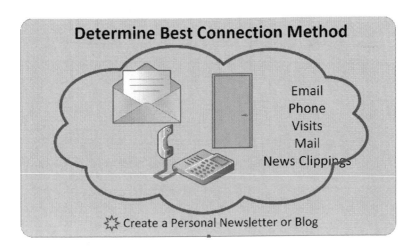

152

that would also not take too much of their time. Ask them if that would be all right. Just about everyone will agree to this.

Next, find out their preferred method of connection. This will vary based on the individual, the time they have available, the distance you are from each other, and other factors.

Your job here is to know how to best communicate with them. There are several ways: e-mail, phone, personal visit, "snail" mail, news updates/clippings, blogs, etc. Let them know you respect them and their accomplishments and you would like to remain connected, but you don't want to be a pest, so you have found a few different methods to provide this communication. Ask which method they would they prefer.

The fact that you will be asking them the best way to reach them will keep you from annoying them. If someone views e-mail as antiquated or impersonal, you might want to offer a call or a visit. For someone extremely busy, you might offer to send them a link to your blog. There are many ways to approach them and offer something of value without feeling like they have just made a lifelong commitment to you.

Understanding their preferred method of communication is not only beneficial but very considerate, as you want to keep potential references informed, but not annoy them.

Share Your Accomplishments

You should be keeping a record of all your activities for your scholarship résumé in your own location or online in Scholarship Keys' Scholarship Résumé Repository. This

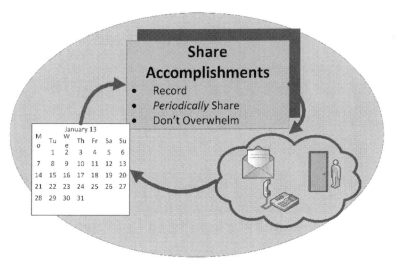

will allow you to more easily share them with your potential references. When you request a reference, you want them to be able to provide concrete examples of why they would recommend you. These examples will come from personal interactions, but by sharing what you are doing on a regular basis, you will get two bonus results that they might include in their recommendations of you.

First, over the months or years that you keep these individuals apprised of the wonderful things that you have achieved, when they read these accomplishments, they will learn of other activities that you have excelled in and they will be able to relate these to their own personal experiences. This will provide them more examples of the particular trait they are striving to convince the committee you possess. For example, say you were applying for a leadership scholarship and the reference you are using is a former teacher. She might be able to speak to how you led a team on a project you worked on. If since that time in the class you became the president of the science club and the lacrosse team captain, she could add these facts as further evidence of your accomplishments in this particular area. If you don't share these accomplishments with your referral sources, they are limited in the experiences they can address on your behalf.

The second area that you gain as a bonus is the recognition that you follow up and thereby can be trusted. Whenever you make and keep a commitment, it strengthens the positive view of you in the eyes of those with whom you made the commitment. While working as the CEO of an international trade association, I interacted with many vice presidents. I am pleased to share that without exception they have been individuals of talent. But when the most talented fails to follow-through on a commitment, the skills which he possesses become diminished in my eyes. When those who perhaps do not have as many talents provide consistent and reliable follow-through on project after project, I find myself trusting them more than one who might actually have more talent. And as a result, I speak more highly of them when asked.

Making the Ask!

When you have done some cultivating of your reference, you should be direct and ask if he is willing to be a reference for you. Ideally, this should be done some time

Willing to Be a Reference?

before you actually need the reference and after you've given a few updates on your accomplishments.

If the answer is no, that's okay . . . it's always a great learning opportunity if someone tells you no. If they don't initially share why they would not be willing to be a reference for you, ask them. The more you know about those who don't want to do this, the better you will know how to adjust your presentation of yourself. If the answer is "no," don't worry; this is why we have been cultivating several potential reference candidates. Just move back to the appropriate step with another of your potential references and start down the flow chart again. Remember to be gracious – you will surely cross paths with them again and you will want the experience to be a positive one.

Assuming the answer is "yes," thank your reference and tell her what form that request will take when the time comes (we will cover this in the next few sections). Let her know that once she writes one reference for you, it might be a good idea to keep a copy of it for ease of potential subsequent reference requests. The reason for this is that you are qualified for several scholarships and as those scholarships ask for references, you would like to provide this reference's name, and you would like to save her the trouble of having to start over when an additional request might come.

Asking for Real!

Now that she has agreed to be a reference for you, you will be keeping her apprised of the various efforts and activities you are involved in. Remember: inform, don't overwhelm.

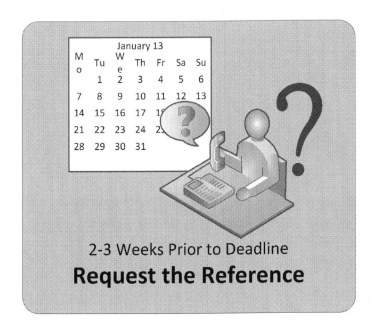

2-3 Weeks Prior to Deadline

Request the Reference

"Asking for real" means that you have an actual application that requires a reference and the individual you have communicated with is a good match for the scholarship you are applying for. When you approach her, remind her of her willingness to be your reference by thanking her for the conversation you had earlier. If circumstances have changed for her and she are no longer willing or able to provide a reference, she will let you know. You don't need to open the door for refusal to provide you a reference by asking again.

The conversation could go something like this:

"Professor Weinstein, thank you again for your willingness to be a reference for me. I have an application for a scholarship that is focused on my academic achievements and I believe you are exactly the kind of person they would like to hear from."

This conversation should occur about 2-3 weeks before the deadline of the scholarship. There are several reasons to provide them ample time. They are doing you a favor, so be considerate of their time. By providing them ample notice, you have shown them that you are the kind of person who plans ahead and can be relied on. This, too, is important because feelings can infuse into in the language we use. The more inconvenience you create for your reference, the less glowing that reference is likely to be.

In the example above, we did more than not ask them a second time for a reference. We assumed that their commitment previously given was still valid. We gave them sincere praise for and recognized their unique qualifications as a reference for this applicant:

"You know my artistic talents better than anyone."

"You have worked with so many talented individuals over the years, so I know you can provide a solid point of reference to the committee."

"As I shared with you before, when I thought of people who know me for who I really am and my potential, you immediately came to mind."

Finally, in that opening greeting, you provided her with some valuable information about the nature of the scholarship; the more specifics you can provide the better. You want your reference to understand the qualities and experiences that when highlighted will enhance your chances of winning the scholarship, so if you don't tell her what the scholarship is being awarded for or what the committee is looking to understand, you increase the chance that such pertinent facts will not be revealed by your reference.

After you have the "real ask" conversation, make sure you follow it up with an e-mail. In that e-mail, reiterate all the things that you said in person. It creates a record that is easy to refer back to in case your reference takes the full three weeks before they can get around to it and have forgotten some of the points you made. In this e-mail, be sure to include any links to the scholarship that might be appropriate, like a link to the scholarship description, a link to the referral information entry page, or a link to your blog or other biographical information on you. If you don't have a link, feel free to provide a brief biographical statement that shares how you are qualified for this scholarship. We will discuss this more in the next section.

Last reminder on making the "real ask": make sure your reference provides you with her best contact information, including her proper title, her name spelled out fully, address, phone number, and position. You might need all of the above and getting this information from your source at this point will reaffirm your confidence that she is committed to providing you a reference.

Simplify Their Life

Keep in mind that some of those you ask will not have written many or any references. The simpler you can make the process, the better:

- Have a brief biographical statement included for them to refer to. This will provide them the correct way to refer to your activities (and even the correct way to spell your name).

- Include sample references that have been written relating to the subject of the scholarship you are applying for.

- Write the first draft. Some folks will want you to provide them some an initial draft of the reference itself. If this is the case for you, make sure it is accurate and correct. It is possible (but not optimal) that they may sign it and just turn it in.

There are a few different ways references can work. The primary one is electronic submission online. Online submission has grown in popularity as nearly everything has

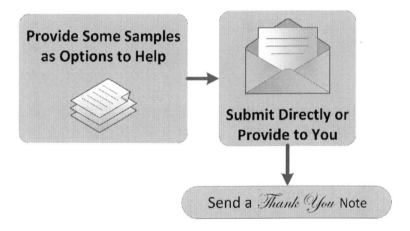

moved online. The benefits of this method are largely for the committee members. They get a nicely consistent format from everyone. There is no misfiling of a letter and they are easily compared one with another both for a given candidate and between two candidates. There is typically a link that is provided or that you will be asked to provide to your reference sources. Once they have successfully completed their electronic submission, a confirmation is usually sent to them and often to the applicant as well.

The second most popular referral method is the written letter. This used to be the only way it could be done, and there were many disadvantages such as lost or misfiled letters. In addition to those shortcomings, if the letter were written by hand, there was also the chance that the handwriting might not be legible. These kinds of referrals do still exist, so be aware and when you encounter a request for one, know what to do. Provide the information to your sources, ask them to type and save their responses (remind them that if another scholarship opportunity arises, this will save them the time of having to recreate their responses from scratch), and provide any postage or envelope properly addressed to the scholarship committee with your request.

The third and less likely referral method is the oral referral. This entails either the entire scholarship committee on a conference call or one of the committee members calling your reference source to ask about your qualifications for the award. The positive side of this is that in light of the time consuming nature of these kinds of requests, you can feel happy that you have likely moved into the finalists' ranks, as the committee will not call the references for every applicant.

Lastly, and most importantly, make sure you thank your reference sources. Thank them when you ask in person, and thank them when you provide them the e-mail with the pertinent information. As mentioned earlier, when submitting an online reference, often these sites will provide you with notification that a reference was received from your source. Thank them for submitting this when you get such a notice as well. Your courtesy encourages them be more open to future reference requests and submissions. As you are going to be submitting a lot of scholarship applications, you want to make sure your sources are perfectly aware of your gratitude.

Summary

The skills and techniques you have learned in this chapter should help you to woo and court solid references that you can use on multiple occasions for several different scholarship applications. Be confident in your ability to answer all of the questions listed below, so you can be sure of the technique to enhance your success.

- Who makes a good reference?

- How to build a portfolio of reference candidates?

- How should you establish contact?

- What's the best way to reach and communicate with your references?

- How can you help them remember and continue to know you?

- What are the best ways of asking them to be a reference for you?

- How to ask them to submit a referral?

- What can you do to help them succeed for you?

- Have you thanked them for what they are doing for you?

Utilizing this method will help you have much better prepared references who will provide you with the best possible referrals. This can help tip the decision in your favor should the competition for an award be close.

CHAPTER 9: 'W' IS FOR WINNER!

Now that you have built your personal version of the Scholarship Résumé . . .

- What you should do with it?
- How do you use your scholarship résumé to win scholarship and award money?
- What kind of money is possible for you?
- When should you start or when is it too late to get scholarships?

Chapter 9: 'W' is for Winner!

Before we get into some of the details of how to go about winning more scholarships using your scholarship résumé, let me share an experience of one young man, his mother, and their scholarship journey. This young man was a good student; not a straight A student, but a good one. He got involved in a number of activities, but wasn't president of his class. He was involved in one sport, played an instrument, and got involved in service activities. He and his mother started applying for scholarships together, and once they had applied to a few, they applied to a few more, and a few more. His mother even kept cutting and pasting his information into forms when he was at school. In the end, he won over fifteen scholarships, the largest of which was worth $20,000! This method works – but like most worthwhile activities, it takes work. Working individually, or together as parents and students with a plan, will get you to the winner's stand on the scholarship front. In this chapter I will share exactly what work you need to do.

apply, Apply, APPLY!

My journalism teacher, Mrs. Rosemary Randolph, used to drill into our heads that the three rules of journalism are: accuracy, Accuracy, ACCURACY! I am not sure that those rules still apply today in the sensationalized, shock value reporting that seems to pervade our news sources, but I would like to borrow from that pithy repetition. The three rules for winning scholarships are: apply, Apply, APPLY!

There are two simple points that I want to make here. There are over three million scholarships worth over sixteen billion dollars offered every year, and your odds increase with every application you make. Let me use a business illustration to make this point.

If you are in the sales business, you need to reach out to as many clients as possible. Not all of those clients will buy what you are selling. That doesn't mean you are not selling a good product – it just means that they either don't want your product at this time, or they don't understand how your amazing product will help them. A good salesperson will not let this discourage her. In fact, great sales people actually get encouraged by these failures. Why do they get encouraged? Because they understand statistics. They come to know that it will take about one hundred cold calls to get an appointment, about three of those ten appointments will be interested, and of those three, they can usually sell to one of them. So for every "no, thank you" they get, they know they are moving forward to the "yes, I'd love one" that will make their month.

You have millions of potential scholarship applications you could submit, so don't get discouraged if you don't win every scholarship you apply for.

My second point is I can't tell you how many people just don't expend the effort to apply.

I know this makes no sense whatsoever, but in my admittedly non-scientific survey of students and their scholarship application habits, I have found that most seniors in high school who have applied for scholarships have applied to anywhere from three to seven and they typically win one to two. Of college students who I ask how many scholarships they have applied to while in college, the overwhelming response is – none!

We all get busy. We all imagine how wonderful it would be if we were to win a scholarship, but way too few actually go through the effort to apply. And here's a not so big secret – if you don't apply for a scholarship, the chances of winning go way down! You have to apply to win! If you have yet to apply for a scholarship, put down this book right now for a few minutes and go through the effort to actually apply for one.

Did you actually stop and go apply? Most people will just blow through this sentence and assure themselves they will go and do that later – and most won't. Those who win multiple scholarships will.

Favorite Application Sites

All right, Dr. Mitchell, I understand that I need to apply, but where do I go to do so?

In this section, I will share some of my favorite sites, but this list does get updated from time to time. For the latest thinking on the "best" sites go to _www.scholarshipkeys.com_ and sign up for our free members' section; this is where I keep some of the most helpful ones listed. There are a few of them that have been around for a while, so let me walk you through some of these most popular ones and what makes them different or the same, so you can decide where the best place for you to start might be.

The website that schools recommend most often, and it is a good one, is ***www.fastweb.com***. It's good because it's free, has a massive database of awards, and features some career planning advice as well. The next site, ***www.scholarships.com***, has literally millions of scholarships as well as college applications available. The site has been around for years, so don't expect it to go away any time soon. Not only is it a reliable place to start searching for the scholarships you would like to apply for, but it will allow you select the scholarships you wish to apply for by your major, year in school, and location.

There are new sites coming on line all the time. The free member section of **Scholarship Keys** is being updated with the sites that we feel are the best resource for you to use.

This Lunch is Always FREE!

This segment is a word of caution. The college market is a huge market with many individuals trying to prey on students as innocent victims. Whenever you apply for a scholarship, NEVER pay to apply for a scholarship or to join a scholarship site! If a site asks you to pay to apply for a scholarship, it is sending a clear message – SCAM! Run away; run away fast.

Every single one of the sites that I mentioned above are free and they have millions of scholarships listed. There is never reason to pay for a scholarship application.

There *is* such a thing as a free lunch. There is no monetary cost for the scholarship free lunch. The cost that you must pay – and it is inevitable for all legitimate scholarship applications – is the time and work to apply.

Possible Application Types

There are tons of scholarship application types that you may be qualified to apply for. Let me just list a few here, so you can get a feeling for what I am referring to. These types I will list here are just the board categories, each of them in turn could also have specializations as well.

Academic	*Community*
Athletics	*Religious*
Fine Arts	*Clubs*
Leadership	*Business*

Let me give you some specific examples on how these categories can be expanded to offer several choices.

Academic: There are several scholarships that want to understand what kind of grade point average (GPA) you received in school. There are also specialized scholarships that will want to know your overall GPA, but will also want to award in a focused area of excellence. For example, if there is a physics scholarship, your overall GPA will be of interest (remember scholarship committees want to be sure that their funds will be well used by a successful student), but they will also look for your specific physics grade, projects you have undertaken, perhaps a science club presentation, and very likely a recommendation from your physics teacher. That is just one subset of academic scholarships that you might be interested in applying for.

Athletics: In the athletics category, specialization is the name of the game. You will not likely get an athletic scholarship for basketball and swimming from the same school. While you will likely need to choose one or the other, you can apply for both at multiple schools (assuming, of course, you can both dribble and butterfly). When applying for these scholarships, your best opportunity is to start early communication with the coaches at the schools you are interested in attending. Your high school coach can help you connect, and that will be critical to your success on this front. Footage and articles demonstrating your prowess in your field will likely be required as well.

This process typically needs to start around your junior year in high school, so you can build a rapport with the coaches and better understand the programs you are applying for.

Fine Arts: There are many different kinds of fine arts that can be leveraged into scholarship opportunities. These include performance (acting, singing, etc.), writing (poems, novels, plays, and more), drawing (graphic design, sketching), sculpture (various media and sizes), music (band, orchestra, vocal, composition), etc. Any one of these has many opportunities both specifically at schools you may be interested in, as well as generally from various foundations or interested parties. Be sure to capture any awards or shows you are a participant in, so you can easily remember all of the experience you have had. For example, if you are a singer, make a record of all your concerts and the pieces you have performed.

Leadership: Leadership scholarships can take a couple of forms. First is the general leadership scholarship. This type is usually designed to provide opportunities for those who have demonstrated leadership qualities in any particular endeavor. You could have been the leader of your church youth group, captain of your team, president of a club, treasurer at a local charity, or all of the above. The second type is actually every other scholarship you might apply for. When you apply for a scholarship, always try to find an opportunity to demonstrate that you have been a leader in some fashion that relates to the scholarship you are applying for: athletics, perhaps you were the captain or share an event that demonstrated leadership; maybe you were president of your fine arts class; you may have held a club leadership position; or, you can show how you helped another group improve.

Community: Service to a charity such as a homeless shelter or a cause like preserving nature is usually well received. Boy or Girl scouts are always good to at least mention and if you have excelled in those organizations, share how you have stood apart from and above the others. You want to show that you have helped make a difference in moving the cause you support forward. If you have a cause that you believe in, but there is no organization that supports such, go back to Chapter 6 on how to set up your own organization. Additionally, if you volunteer at a larger charity (Red Cross or American Cancer Society, for example), there may be scholarships they offer directly as well.

Religious: There are religion-specific scholarships that are intended to benefit students of a particular religion. Additionally, some faith-based schools offer scholarships to entice students of similar faith to attend their institution. In addition to the obvious religion scholarships, there is another opportunity that many miss. If you are a regular churchgoer, on most scholarship applications, that is considered community service. The hours spent doing good with your church or congregation can be tracked and shared as hours of service. Leadership positions at church, missionary service, and assisting the poor and needy are all experiences to be highlighted for service-based scholarships or scholarships that have an interest in service that has been rendered. Keep track of your church time, it can help you in material ways as well as spiritual ones.

Clubs: There are many clubs that are available for a student to get involved in during high school or college. Each one you participate in will help further flesh out your scholarship résumé. As shared earlier, you can also create a club and become its president to add to the leadership portion of your scholarship résumé. And as you will discover below, there are specialty scholarships that a particular club might help you win. In addition to the clubs that students join at school, there are external clubs that provide scholarships as well. Your local Rotary, Lions, or Jaycee organizations often have scholarship monies set aside for those in their communities. Even your local Chamber of Commerce may have scholarships, so be sure to enquire about them.

Business: More and more banks, credit unions, utilities companies, parents' employers, local businesses, and local philanthropic pillars of the community offer scholarships. Most students don't even think about going to their electric company or bank to apply for a scholarship, but many companies have them.

There are more types than I could possibly list, but I have tried to develop a list of several that will get you thinking and hopefully spur you on to several additional categories that you might not have pursued or even considered before. It is available for free download at *www.scholarshipresume.com*.

Odd and Quirky Scholarships

In addition to those various broad types of scholarships mentioned above, there are several "specialty" scholarships. I was initially surprised by many of these, but there are so many quirky scholarships available now that I thought it would be worth sharing several that I have seen to get you thinking whether something like these might be applicable to you.

Social Media, chess, juggling, skateboarding, performing magic, really any "talent" you might have are all potential areas for scholarships. I haven't found the Tiddlywinks scholarship yet; someone let me know if you find one.

While none of these may apply to you, you might find that you have other skills that may have scholarships available for you. Best of luck in finding a way to help pay off your college experience with your unique talent or interest area. Frisbee, anyone?

Twice a Day Keeps the Loans at Bay!

You can optimize the scholarship application process (and that is one of the main points of creating your scholarship résumé) so that you are able to apply to a scholarship in about fifteen minutes. And if you set a goal of applying for thirty minutes a day, you could apply about two hundred scholarships over a single semester! That would be the equivalent of giving you twenty times more chances of winning than the typical over-achiever applying from high school (the good high school student will apply to five scholarships and most over-achievers apply for about ten). If you are a college student doing this, you are way ahead of the game. As I shared earlier, even the honor students that I worked with and begged to apply for scholarships, as a general rule – didn't.

How can you possibly do two applications a day? Let me attempt to draw a parallel to your brain. The brain functions through synapses firing. The more connections you have to a given memory, the more likely that that memory cell will be able to be accessed. In the scholarship world, the more connections you make to various scholarships, the more likely you will be to gain access to or win a given scholarship. And the more you apply for, the easier and more proficient you become at it.

Develop strategies like applying for only service scholarships one week. Once you do two or three, the rest get pretty easy as they are all very similar. Then the next week, do your leadership scholarships and so on. Using your scholarship résumé and practicing techniques like this will allow you to apply to at least two a day. It may seem like a lot of work, but if you could win ten scholarships from that effort of one semester (winning one out of twenty applied for), would an extra $10,000 tax-free be worth your time? Do the math. That is the equivalent of making $200 an hour! Not many students are generating that kind of return on the time they spend. Take the time.

Systemize Your Winning!

Hearing something that makes sense is nice. Learning it so that it is yours – even better. Actually changing your behavior based on what you have learned – priceless! It has been my experience when attending a lecture or reading a book that is designed to help me, that in the moment, I think, "I really should be doing this." However, with the daily busyness that we all face, those great intentions usually fall by the wayside. Understanding this, we have developed the Full Ride Scholarship Program that we offer with a money back guarantee to help everyone "Eliminate College Costs" and be more successful in their university endeavors.

The *Full Ride Scholarship Program* provides video clips, articles, reference points, insights to successful use of the Scholarship Résumé, and an Accountability System that helps you with reminders and motivators to do all the things that will help you eliminate college costs and make getting your college education less costly. And because you purchased this book, we will give you a $30 credit when you sign up for the annual program. In the coupon code or discount code field when checking out, just enter <u>SRES30</u> for your discount to the program!

This program also incorporates the Scholarship Résumé Repository. It will allow you to store all of your information that has been described in this book in a single location in the cloud and allow you to more easily apply for at least two scholarships a day.

In Conclusion

Well, you stuck through to the end! Well done! You have several valuable tools that have been shared in this book, and now that you own it, feel free to reference it when you forget exactly how to build up your scholarship résumé.

Your education is incalculably valuable, but that doesn't mean you shouldn't do everything you can to reduce or eliminate costs that are associated with it. Developing your own personal version of the Scholarship Résumé will help you be more efficient and effective in winning your share of the billions of dollars in scholarships that are available to you.

ABOUT THE AUTHOR

Always involved in education, Dr. John W. Mitchell is a thought leader on various aspects of advancing and resolving education issues. He has done this in his current role as IPC's president and CEO, Dr. John W. Mitchell (joining in 2012) where he has championed IPC programs such as a new learning management platform, IPC EDGE; an Online Certification Portal; and a re-engineered Member Success department.

Dr. Mitchell began as an engineer at General Electric Aerospace in 1988. In 1992, he joined Alpine Electronics and became a founding member of its research company which is credited for introducing navigation systems to the U.S. OEM market. During his tenure at Alpine, he held several positions, including manager of software engineering, director of IT and senior director of strategic planning. Mitchell also was awarded a patent in the vehicle navigation space while at Alpine.

In 2003, Dr. Mitchell was recruited to Bose Corporation where he served as general manager/director of a new global business unit – Bose's largest-ever product development initiative. Just prior to joining IPC, he served as the CEO of Golden Key International Honour Society, the world's premier collegiate honor society, with more than 2 million members from more than 190 nations where he stabilized the organization fiscally and multiplied the scholarships by four times to over $1 million awarded in a single year.

Dr. Mitchell's academic credentials include a doctorate in higher education management from University of Georgia's Institute of Higher Education; a Master of Business Administration from Pepperdine University and a Bachelor of Science in electrical and computer engineering from Brigham Young University.

In his spare time, he enjoys triathlons, reading, spending time with his family, and helping students find ways to be successful in their education objectives.

NOTES & REFERENCES

To download original materials listed in this work, as well as other helpful resources go to:

www.scholarshipresume.com

A few of the items you will find available by going to the above link include:

- Reference Development flow chart
- Passion Worksheet
- *Starting a New Venture* flow diagram
- Links to favorite scholarship aggregators' sites
- Essay Do's & Don'ts, and
- Many other links to resources

[i] San Diego, CA: Building Industry Association. *Four Hour House*. 2004 (DVD).

[ii] *What Will I Need to Fill out the FAFSA?*, United States Department of Education, fafsa.ed.gov/help/before003.htm.

[iii] Hadad, Roxana. "Sample Essay Questions for College Apps." *Fastweb - College Essays*. Fastweb.com, 09 Mar. 2009. Web. 02 Oct. 2013. <http://www.fastweb.com/college-search/articles/sample-essay-questions-for-college-apps>.

[iv] Originally the List of Persuasive Words was found on the University of Maryland's website, now it can be found at: professorarce.weebly.com/uploads/1/3/9/0/13906478/persuasive_vocabulary_list.pdf

[v] Mehrabian, Albert. *Silent Messages: Implicit Communication of Emotions and Attitudes*. Wadsworth, 1977.

Made in the USA
Columbia, SC
28 June 2018